# Walt Disney's Donald Duck

## Flying High

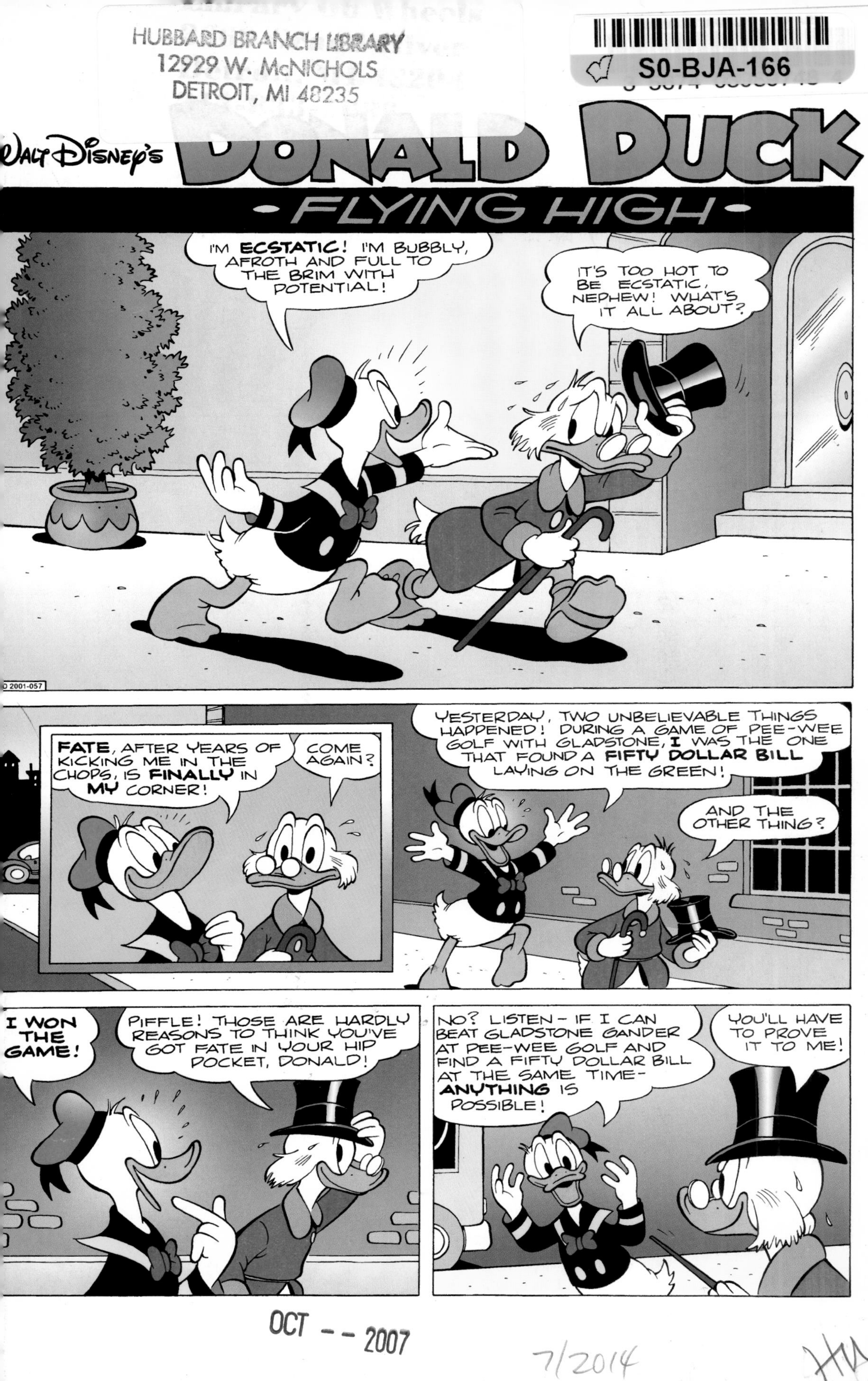
I'M ECSTATIC! I'M BUBBLY, AFROTH AND FULL TO THE BRIM WITH POTENTIAL!
IT'S TOO HOT TO BE ECSTATIC, NEPHEW! WHAT'S IT ALL ABOUT?
D 2001-057
FATE, AFTER YEARS OF KICKING ME IN THE CHOPS, IS FINALLY IN MY CORNER!
COME AGAIN?
YESTERDAY, TWO UNBELIEVABLE THINGS HAPPENED! DURING A GAME OF PEE-WEE GOLF WITH GLADSTONE, I WAS THE ONE THAT FOUND A FIFTY DOLLAR BILL LAYING ON THE GREEN!
AND THE OTHER THING?
I WON THE GAME!
PIFFLE! THOSE ARE HARDLY REASONS TO THINK YOU'VE GOT FATE IN YOUR HIP POCKET, DONALD!
NO? LISTEN - IF I CAN BEAT GLADSTONE GANDER AT PEE-WEE GOLF AND FIND A FIFTY DOLLAR BILL AT THE SAME TIME- ANYTHING IS POSSIBLE!
YOU'LL HAVE TO PROVE IT TO ME!

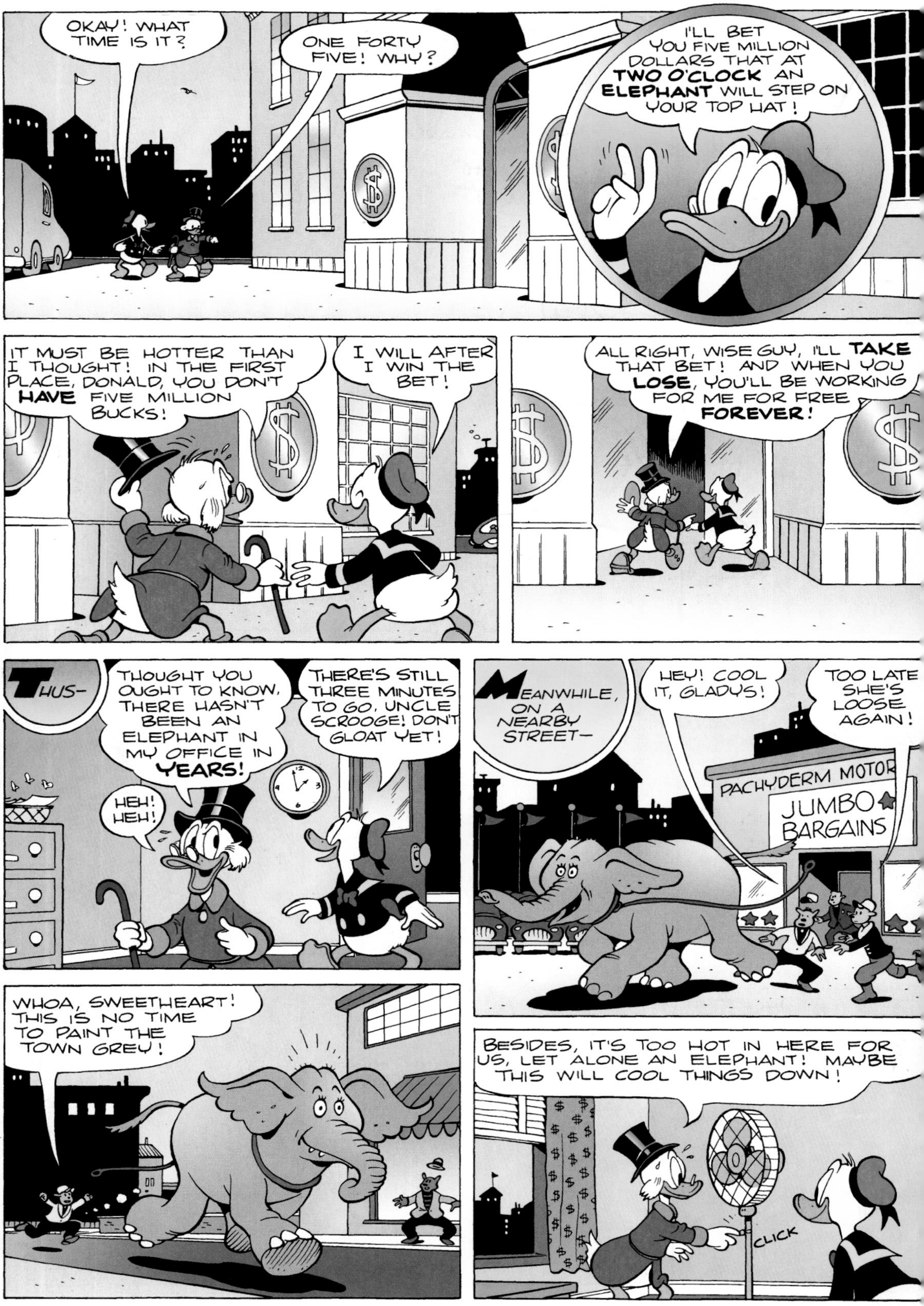
OKAY! WHAT TIME IS IT?
ONE FORTY FIVE! WHY?
I'LL BET YOU FIVE MILLION DOLLARS THAT AT **TWO O'CLOCK** AN **ELEPHANT** WILL STEP ON YOUR TOP HAT!
IT MUST BE HOTTER THAN I THOUGHT! IN THE FIRST PLACE, DONALD, YOU DON'T **HAVE** FIVE MILLION BUCKS!
I WILL AFTER I WIN THE BET!
ALL RIGHT, WISE GUY, I'LL **TAKE** THAT BET! AND WHEN YOU **LOSE**, YOU'LL BE WORKING FOR ME FOR FREE **FOREVER**!
THUS—
THOUGHT YOU OUGHT TO KNOW, THERE HASN'T BEEN AN ELEPHANT IN MY OFFICE IN **YEARS!**
THERE'S STILL THREE MINUTES TO GO, UNCLE SCROOGE! DON'T GLOAT YET!
HEH! HEH!
MEANWHILE, ON A NEARBY STREET—
HEY! COOL IT, GLADYS!
TOO LATE SHE'S LOOSE AGAIN!
PACHYDERM MOTOR
JUMBO BARGAINS
WHOA, SWEETHEART! THIS IS NO TIME TO PAINT THE TOWN GREY!
BESIDES, IT'S TOO HOT IN HERE FOR US, LET ALONE AN ELEPHANT! MAYBE THIS WILL COOL THINGS DOWN!
CLICK

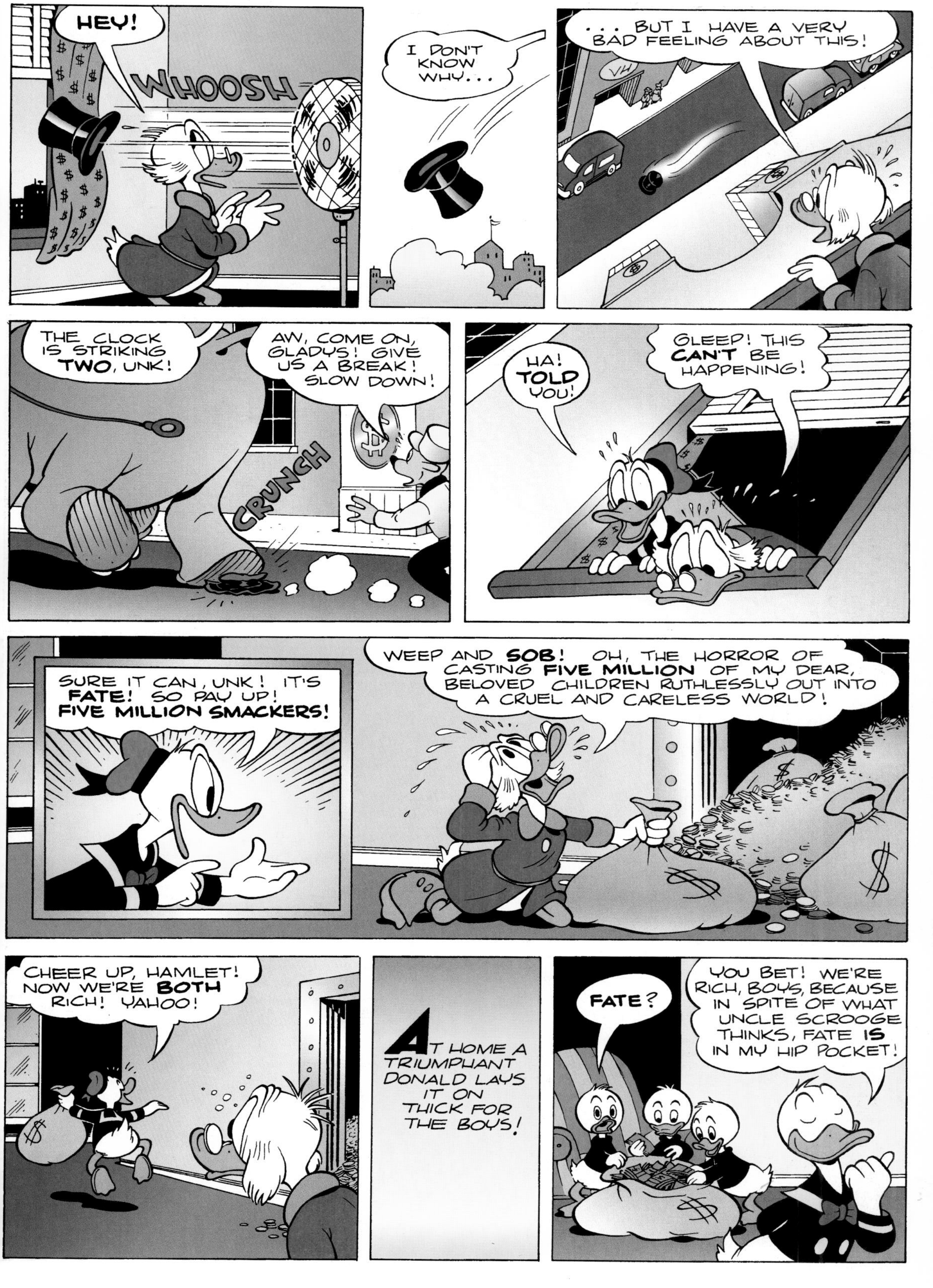
HEY!
WHOOSH
I DON'T KNOW WHY...
... BUT I HAVE A VERY BAD FEELING ABOUT THIS!
THE CLOCK IS STRIKING TWO, UNK!
AW, COME ON, GLADYS! GIVE US A BREAK! SLOW DOWN!
CRUNCH
HA! TOLD YOU!
GLEEP! THIS CAN'T BE HAPPENING!
SURE IT CAN, UNK! IT'S FATE! SO PAY UP! FIVE MILLION SMACKERS!
WEEP AND SOB! OH, THE HORROR OF CASTING FIVE MILLION OF MY DEAR, BELOVED CHILDREN RUTHLESSLY OUT INTO A CRUEL AND CARELESS WORLD!
CHEER UP, HAMLET! NOW WE'RE BOTH RICH! YAHOO!
AT HOME A TRIUMPHANT DONALD LAYS IT ON THICK FOR THE BOYS!
FATE?
YOU BET! WE'RE RICH, BOYS, BECAUSE IN SPITE OF WHAT UNCLE SCROOGE THINKS, FATE IS IN MY HIP POCKET!

35674039897484

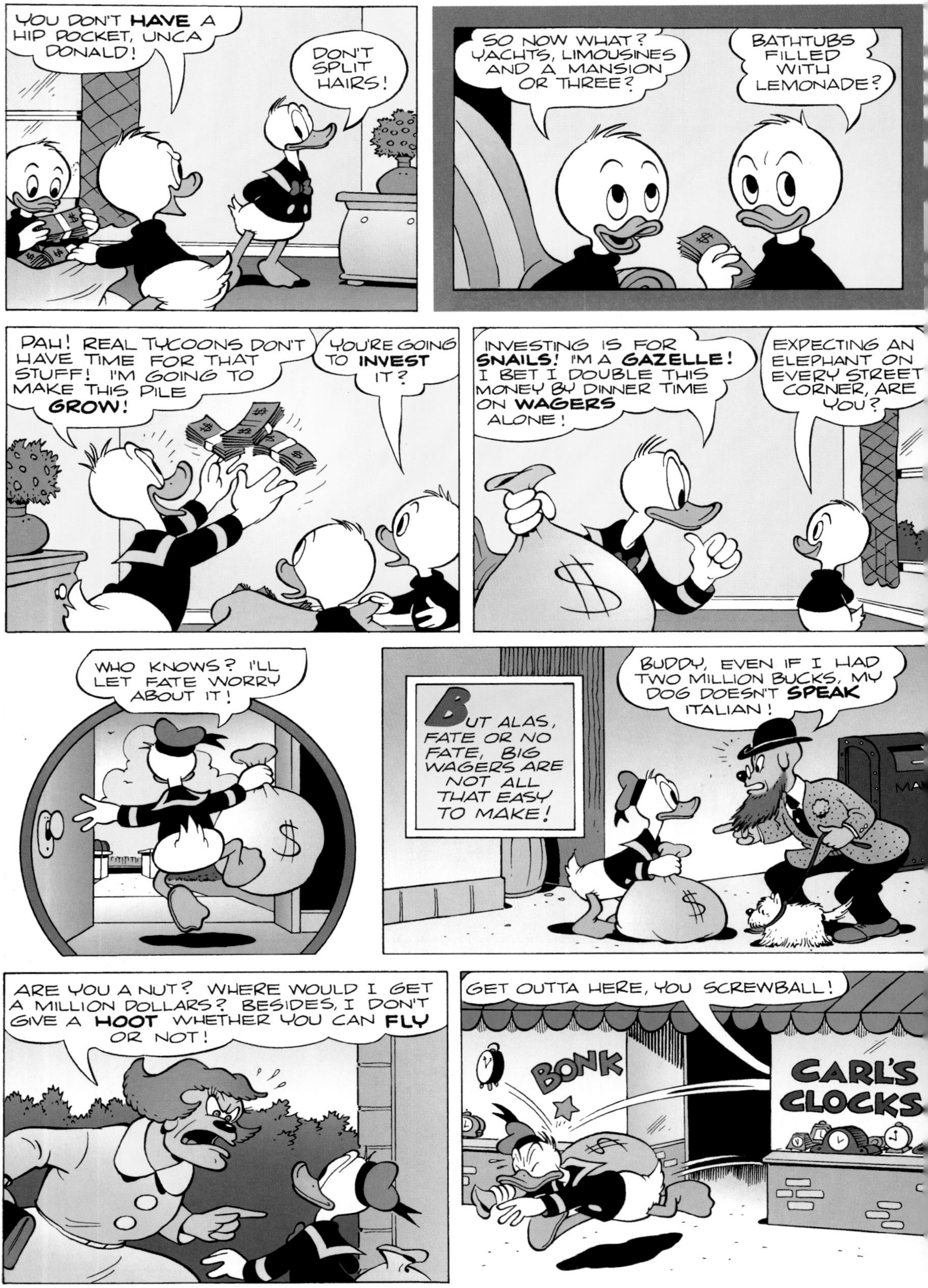
YOU DON'T HAVE A HIP POCKET, UNCA DONALD!
DON'T SPLIT HAIRS!
SO NOW WHAT? YACHTS, LIMOUSINES AND A MANSION OR THREE?
BATHTUBS FILLED WITH LEMONADE?
PAH! REAL TYCOONS DON'T HAVE TIME FOR THAT STUFF! I'M GOING TO MAKE THIS PILE GROW!
YOU'RE GOING TO INVEST IT?
INVESTING IS FOR SNAILS! I'M A GAZELLE! I BET I DOUBLE THIS MONEY BY DINNER TIME ON WAGERS ALONE!
EXPECTING AN ELEPHANT ON EVERY STREET CORNER, ARE YOU?
WHO KNOWS? I'LL LET FATE WORRY ABOUT IT!
BUT ALAS, FATE OR NO FATE, BIG WAGERS ARE NOT ALL THAT EASY TO MAKE!
BUDDY, EVEN IF I HAD TWO MILLION BUCKS, MY DOG DOESN'T SPEAK ITALIAN!
ARE YOU A NUT? WHERE WOULD I GET A MILLION DOLLARS? BESIDES, I DON'T GIVE A HOOT WHETHER YOU CAN FLY OR NOT!
GET OUTTA HERE, YOU SCREWBALL!
BONK
CARL'S CLOCKS

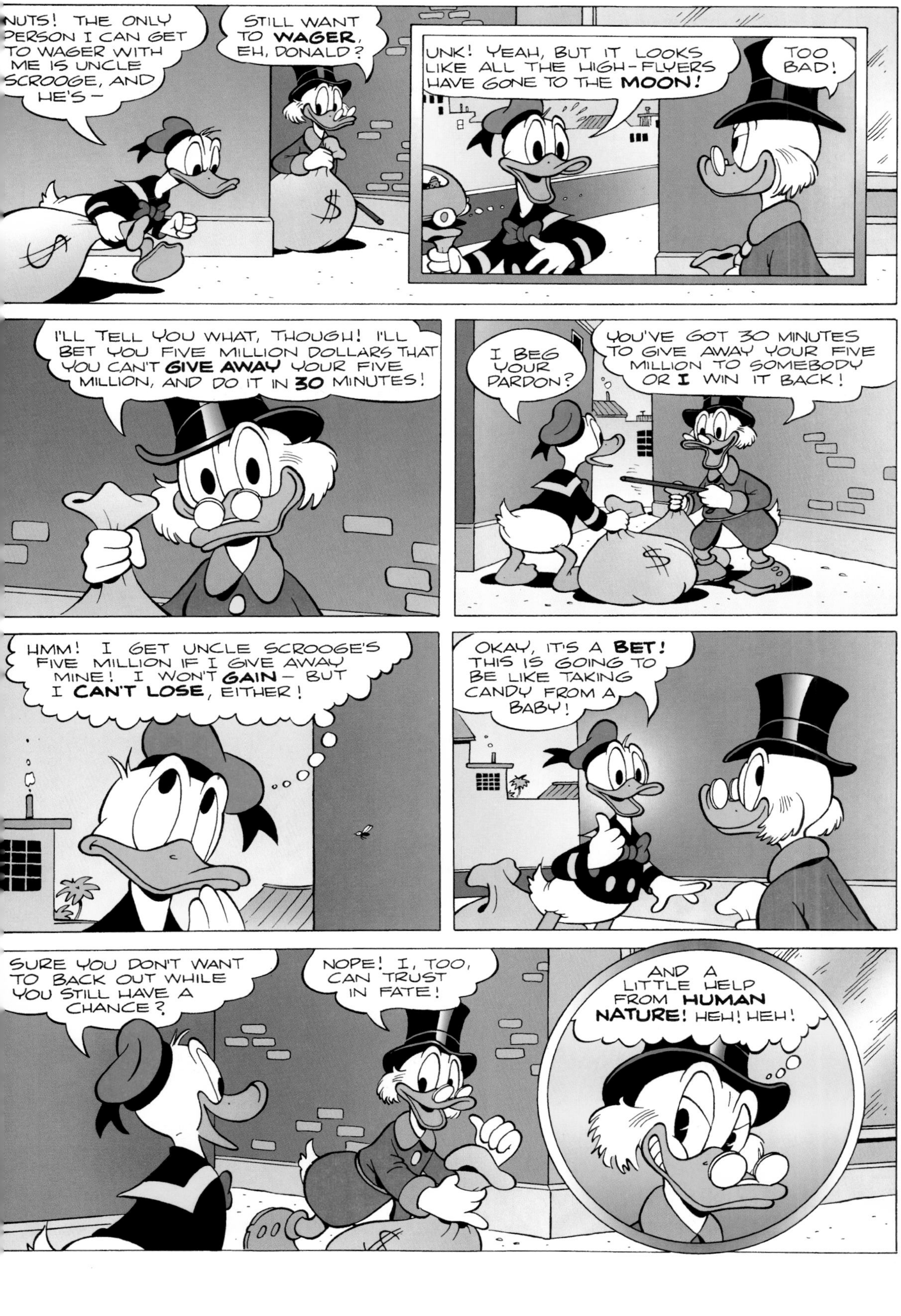
NUTS! THE ONLY PERSON I CAN GET TO WAGER WITH ME IS UNCLE SCROOGE, AND HE'S –
STILL WANT TO **WAGER**, EH, DONALD?
UNK! YEAH, BUT IT LOOKS LIKE ALL THE HIGH-FLYERS HAVE GONE TO THE **MOON**!
TOO BAD!
I'LL TELL YOU WHAT, THOUGH! I'LL BET YOU FIVE MILLION DOLLARS THAT YOU CAN'T **GIVE AWAY** YOUR FIVE MILLION, AND DO IT IN **30** MINUTES!
I BEG YOUR PARDON?
YOU'VE GOT 30 MINUTES TO GIVE AWAY YOUR FIVE MILLION TO SOMEBODY OR **I** WIN IT BACK!
HMM! I GET UNCLE SCROOGE'S FIVE MILLION IF I GIVE AWAY MINE! I WON'T **GAIN** – BUT I **CAN'T LOSE**, EITHER!
OKAY, IT'S A **BET**! THIS IS GOING TO BE LIKE TAKING CANDY FROM A BABY!
SURE YOU DON'T WANT TO BACK OUT WHILE YOU STILL HAVE A CHANCE?
NOPE! I, TOO, CAN TRUST IN FATE!
AND A LITTLE HELP FROM **HUMAN NATURE**! HEH! HEH!

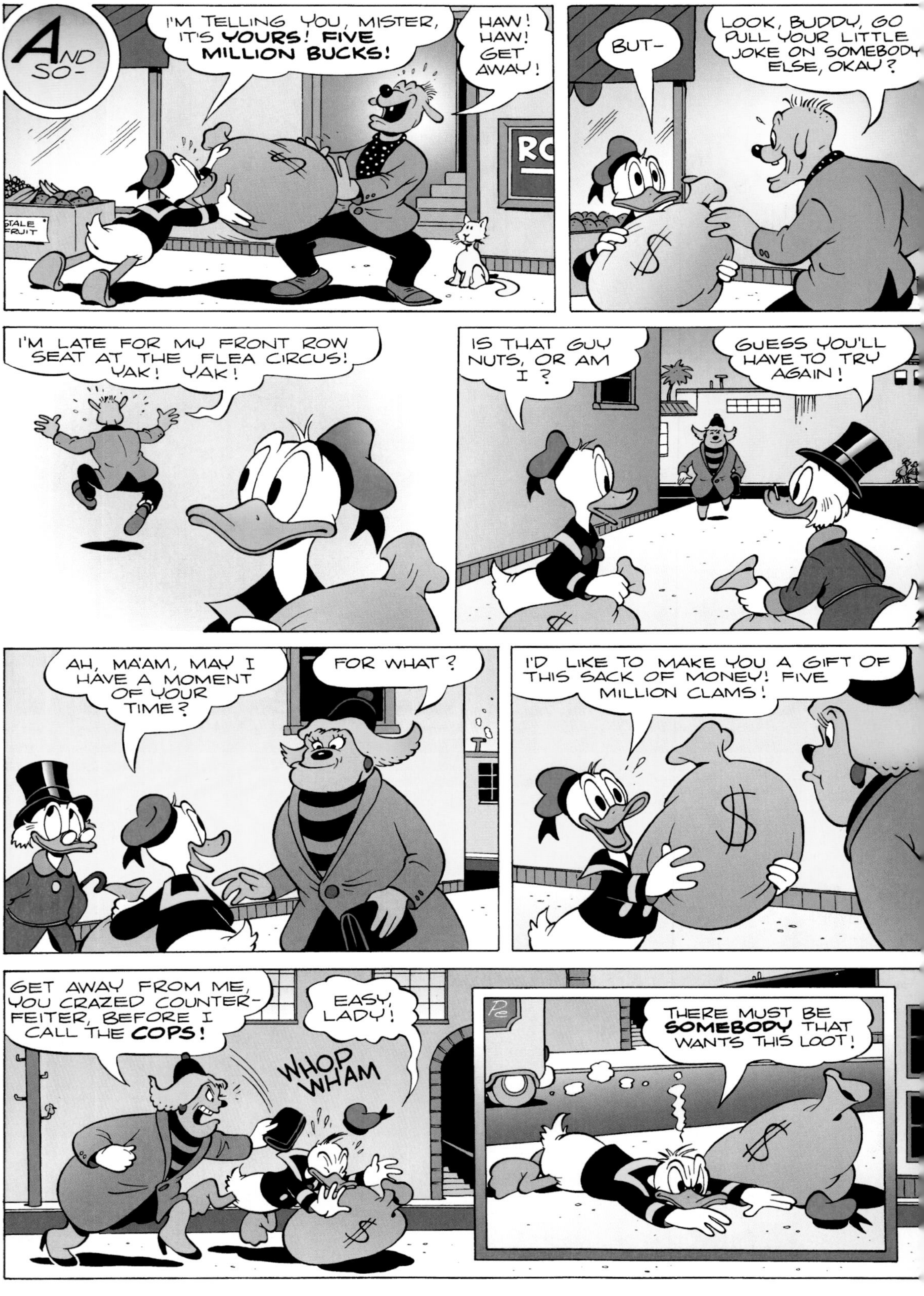
AND SO-
I'M TELLING YOU, MISTER, IT'S **YOURS! FIVE MILLION BUCKS!**
HAW! HAW! GET AWAY!
STALE FRUIT
BUT-
LOOK, BUDDY, GO PULL YOUR LITTLE JOKE ON SOMEBODY ELSE, OKAY?
I'M LATE FOR MY FRONT ROW SEAT AT THE FLEA CIRCUS! YAK! YAK!
IS THAT GUY NUTS, OR AM I?
GUESS YOU'LL HAVE TO TRY AGAIN!
AH, MA'AM, MAY I HAVE A MOMENT OF YOUR TIME?
FOR WHAT?
I'D LIKE TO MAKE YOU A GIFT OF THIS SACK OF MONEY! FIVE MILLION CLAMS!
GET AWAY FROM ME, YOU CRAZED COUNTER-FEITER, BEFORE I CALL THE **COPS!**
EASY, LADY!
WHOP WHAM
THERE MUST BE **SOMEBODY** THAT WANTS THIS LOOT!

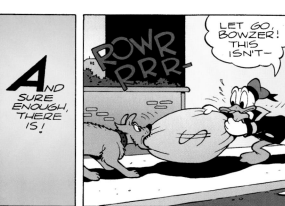

AND SURE ENOUGH, THERE IS!

ROWR RRR—

LET GO, BOWZER! THIS ISN'T—

HEY, UNCLE SCROOGE! DOES GIVING THE MONEY TO A **DOG** COUNT?

AFRAID NOT, DONALD! NICE TRY THOUGH!

OKAY, WOLF FACE! YOU'RE WASTING MY TIME!

ROWR

OKAY! WHO'S **NEXT**?

YOU BETTER HOPE IT'S THAT PANHANDLER, DONALD! YOU'RE DOWN TO 13½ MINUTES!

BUT ALAS—

WHOA THERE, CHARLIE! ALL I WANT IS THE PRICE OF A CUP OF **COFFEE**!

BUT THIS IS FIVE **MILLION** DOLLARS!

WHAT ARE YA TRYIN' T' **DO**, BUCKY? RUIN MY **REPUTATION**?

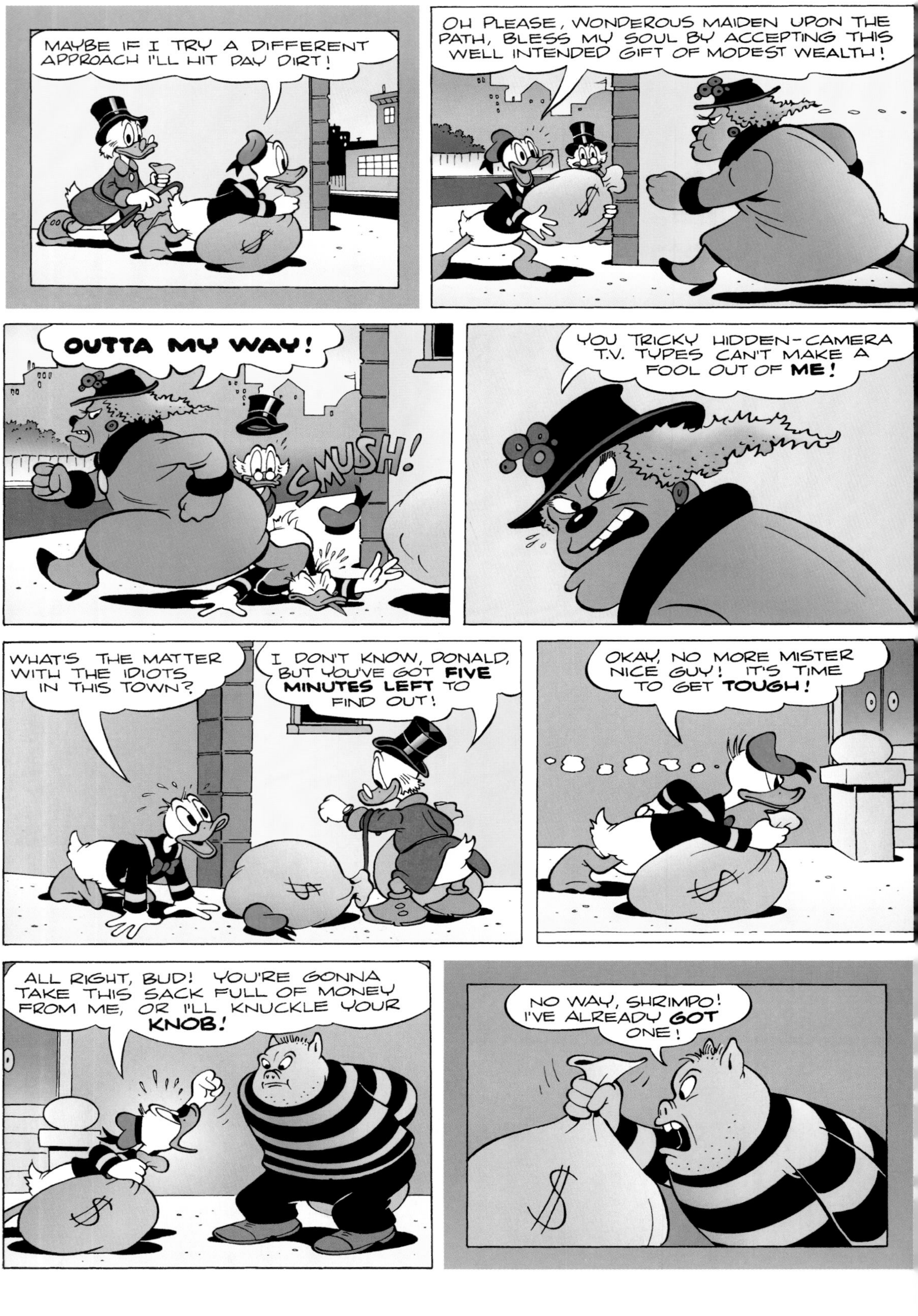

MAYBE IF I TRY A DIFFERENT APPROACH I'LL HIT PAY DIRT!
OH PLEASE, WONDEROUS MAIDEN UPON THE PATH, BLESS MY SOUL BY ACCEPTING THIS WELL INTENDED GIFT OF MODEST WEALTH!
OUTTA MY WAY!
SMUSH!
YOU TRICKY HIDDEN-CAMERA T.V. TYPES CAN'T MAKE A FOOL OUT OF **ME**!
WHAT'S THE MATTER WITH THE IDIOTS IN THIS TOWN?
I DON'T KNOW, DONALD, BUT YOU'VE GOT **FIVE MINUTES LEFT** TO FIND OUT!
OKAY, NO MORE MISTER NICE GUY! IT'S TIME TO GET **TOUGH**!
ALL RIGHT, BUD! YOU'RE GONNA TAKE THIS SACK FULL OF MONEY FROM ME, OR I'LL KNUCKLE YOUR **KNOB**!
NO WAY, SHRIMPO! I'VE ALREADY **GOT** ONE!

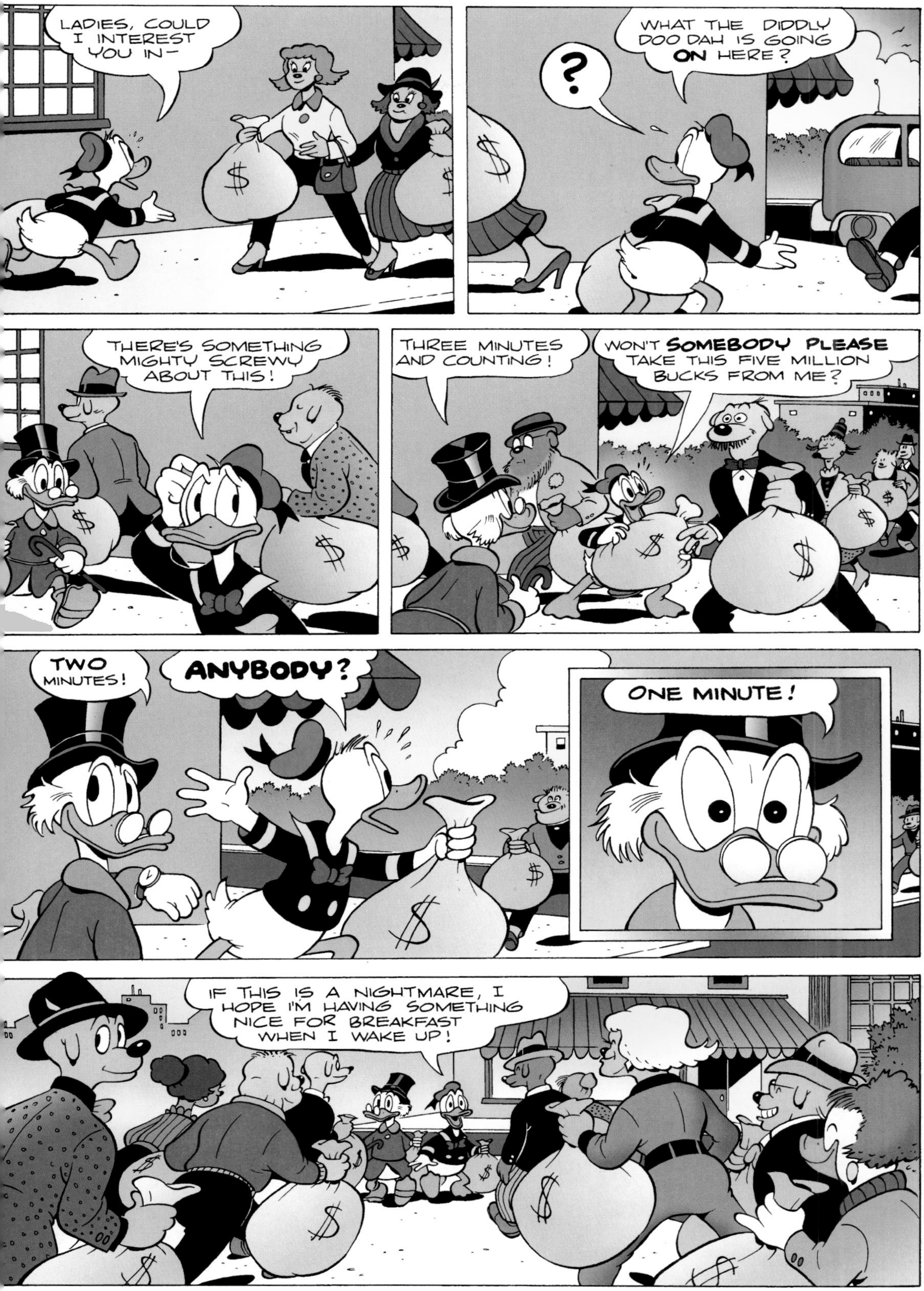
LADIES, COULD I INTEREST YOU IN—
?
WHAT THE DIDDLY DOO DAH IS GOING **ON** HERE?
THERE'S SOMETHING MIGHTY SCREWY ABOUT THIS!
THREE MINUTES AND COUNTING!
WON'T **SOMEBODY PLEASE** TAKE THIS FIVE MILLION BUCKS FROM ME?
TWO MINUTES!
ANYBODY?
ONE MINUTE!
IF THIS IS A NIGHTMARE, I HOPE I'M HAVING SOMETHING NICE FOR BREAKFAST WHEN I WAKE UP!

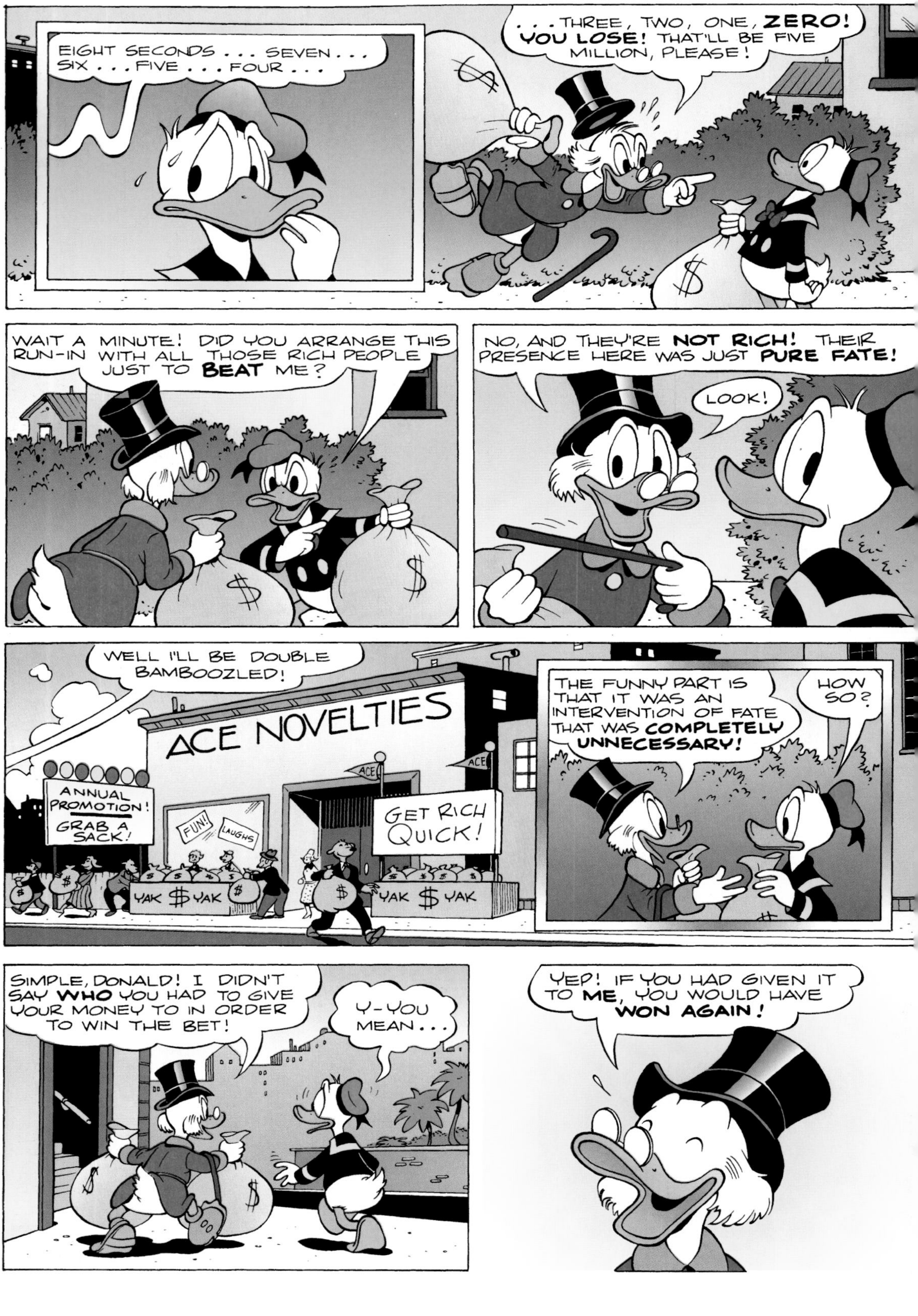
EIGHT SECONDS . . . SEVEN . . . SIX . . . FIVE . . . FOUR . . .
. . . THREE, TWO, ONE, ZERO! YOU LOSE! THAT'LL BE FIVE MILLION, PLEASE!
WAIT A MINUTE! DID YOU ARRANGE THIS RUN-IN WITH ALL THOSE RICH PEOPLE JUST TO BEAT ME?
NO, AND THEY'RE NOT RICH! THEIR PRESENCE HERE WAS JUST PURE FATE!
LOOK!
WELL I'LL BE DOUBLE BAMBOOZLED!
ACE NOVELTIES
ANNUAL PROMOTION! GRAB A SACK!
FUN!
LAUGHS
ACE
ACE
GET RICH QUICK!
YAK $ YAK
YAK $ YAK
THE FUNNY PART IS THAT IT WAS AN INTERVENTION OF FATE THAT WAS COMPLETELY UNNECESSARY!
HOW SO?
SIMPLE, DONALD! I DIDN'T SAY WHO YOU HAD TO GIVE YOUR MONEY TO IN ORDER TO WIN THE BET!
Y-YOU MEAN . . .
YEP! IF YOU HAD GIVEN IT TO ME, YOU WOULD HAVE WON AGAIN!

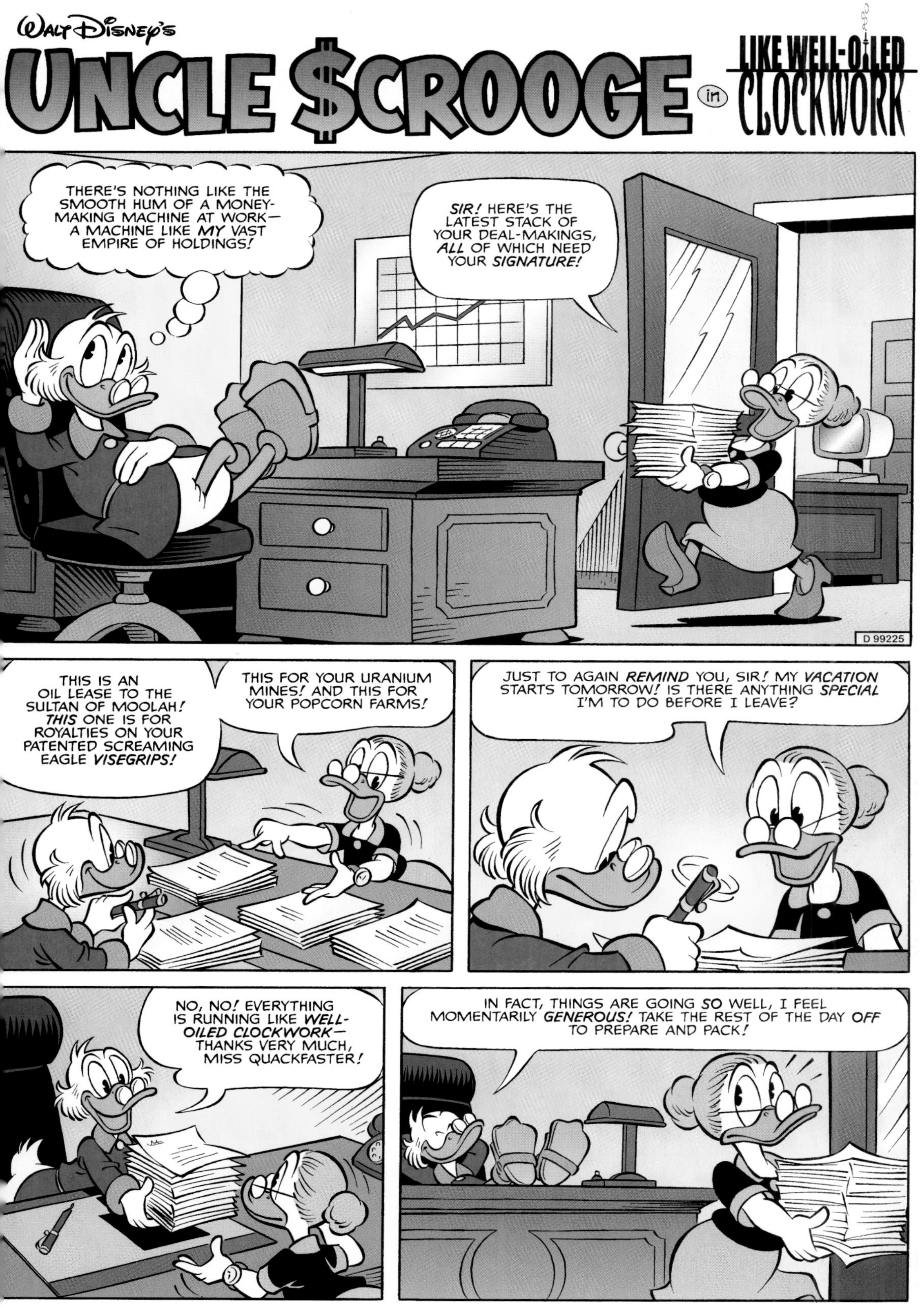
WALT DISNEY'S
UNCLE $CROOGE in LIKE WELL-OILED CLOCKWORK
THERE'S NOTHING LIKE THE SMOOTH HUM OF A MONEY-MAKING MACHINE AT WORK— A MACHINE LIKE MY VAST EMPIRE OF HOLDINGS!
SIR! HERE'S THE LATEST STACK OF YOUR DEAL-MAKINGS, ALL OF WHICH NEED YOUR SIGNATURE!
D 99225
THIS IS AN OIL LEASE TO THE SULTAN OF MOOLAH! THIS ONE IS FOR ROYALTIES ON YOUR PATENTED SCREAMING EAGLE VISEGRIPS!
THIS FOR YOUR URANIUM MINES! AND THIS FOR YOUR POPCORN FARMS!
JUST TO AGAIN REMIND YOU, SIR! MY VACATION STARTS TOMORROW! IS THERE ANYTHING SPECIAL I'M TO DO BEFORE I LEAVE?
NO, NO! EVERYTHING IS RUNNING LIKE WELL-OILED CLOCKWORK— THANKS VERY MUCH, MISS QUACKFASTER!
IN FACT, THINGS ARE GOING SO WELL, I FEEL MOMENTARILY GENEROUS! TAKE THE REST OF THE DAY OFF TO PREPARE AND PACK!

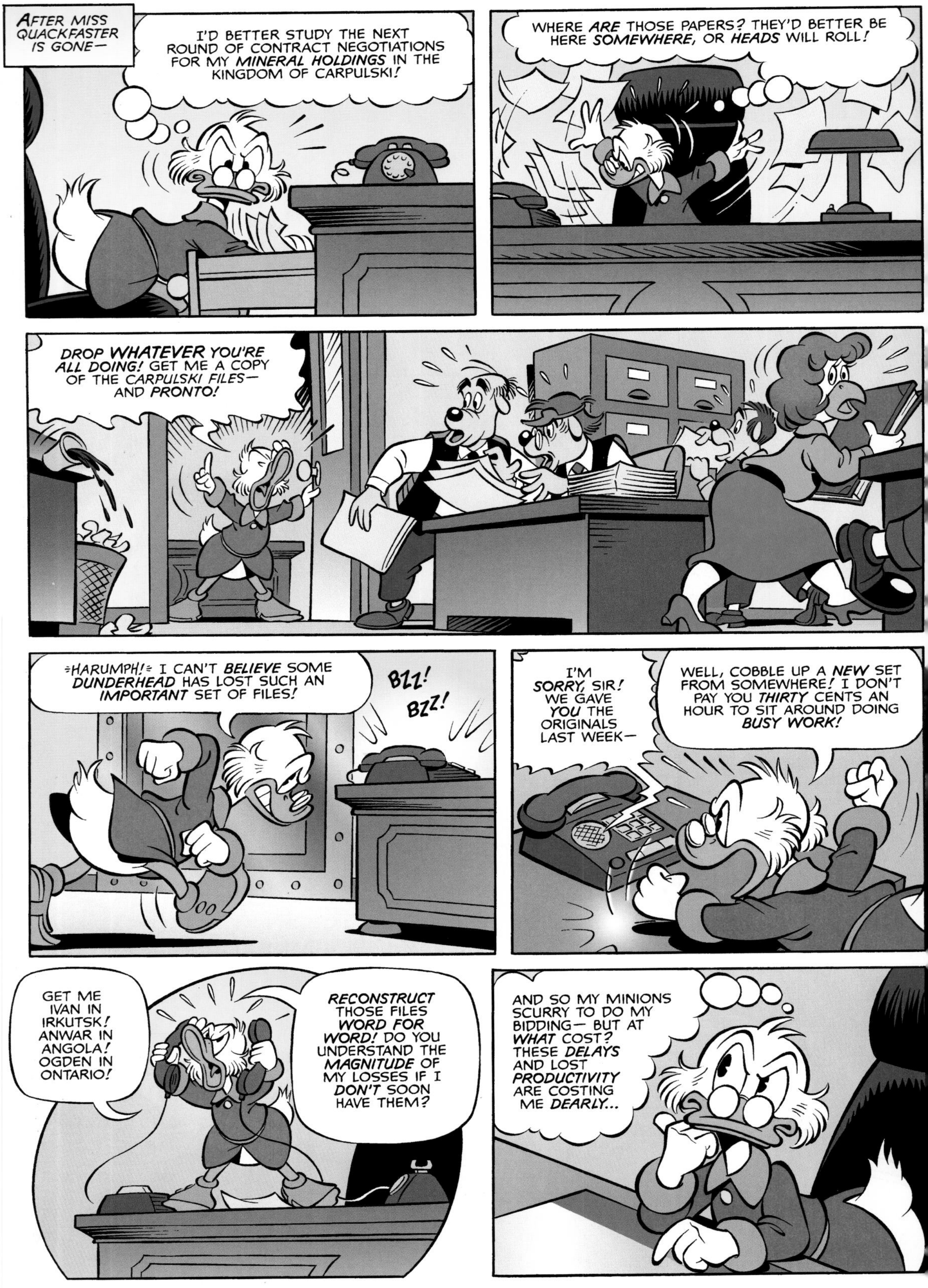
AFTER MISS QUACKFASTER IS GONE—
I'D BETTER STUDY THE NEXT ROUND OF CONTRACT NEGOTIATIONS FOR MY *MINERAL HOLDINGS* IN THE KINGDOM OF CARPULSKI!
WHERE *ARE* THOSE PAPERS? THEY'D BETTER BE HERE *SOMEWHERE*, OR *HEADS* WILL ROLL!
DROP **WHATEVER** YOU'RE *ALL DOING!* GET ME A COPY OF THE CARPULSKI FILES— AND *PRONTO!*
=HARUMPH!= I CAN'T *BELIEVE* SOME *DUNDERHEAD* HAS LOST SUCH AN *IMPORTANT* SET OF FILES!
BZZ! BZZ!
I'M *SORRY*, SIR! WE GAVE *YOU* THE ORIGINALS LAST WEEK—
WELL, COBBLE UP A *NEW* SET FROM SOMEWHERE! I DON'T PAY YOU *THIRTY* CENTS AN HOUR TO SIT AROUND DOING *BUSY WORK!*
GET ME IVAN IN IRKUTSK! ANWAR IN ANGOLA! OGDEN IN ONTARIO!
*RECONSTRUCT* THOSE FILES *WORD FOR WORD!* DO YOU UNDERSTAND THE *MAGNITUDE* OF MY LOSSES IF I *DON'T* SOON HAVE THEM?
AND SO MY MINIONS SCURRY TO DO MY BIDDING— BUT AT *WHAT* COST? THESE *DELAYS* AND LOST *PRODUCTIVITY* ARE COSTING ME *DEARLY...*

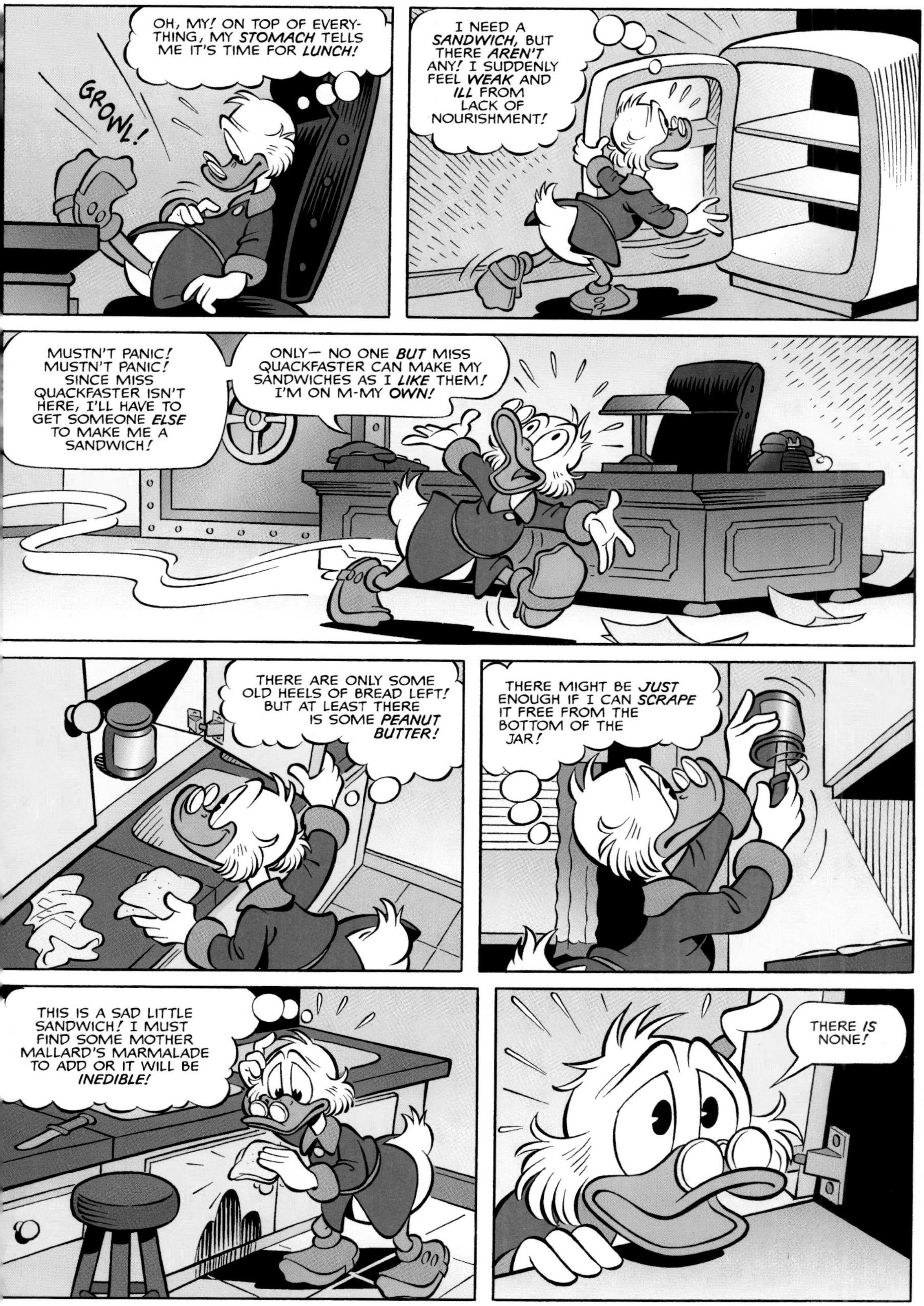
OH, MY! ON TOP OF EVERY-THING, MY STOMACH TELLS ME IT'S TIME FOR LUNCH!
GROWL!
I NEED A SANDWICH, BUT THERE AREN'T ANY! I SUDDENLY FEEL WEAK AND ILL FROM LACK OF NOURISHMENT!
MUSTN'T PANIC! MUSTN'T PANIC! SINCE MISS QUACKFASTER ISN'T HERE, I'LL HAVE TO GET SOMEONE ELSE TO MAKE ME A SANDWICH!
ONLY— NO ONE BUT MISS QUACKFASTER CAN MAKE MY SANDWICHES AS I LIKE THEM! I'M ON M-MY OWN!
THERE ARE ONLY SOME OLD HEELS OF BREAD LEFT! BUT AT LEAST THERE IS SOME PEANUT BUTTER!
THERE MIGHT BE JUST ENOUGH IF I CAN SCRAPE IT FREE FROM THE BOTTOM OF THE JAR!
THIS IS A SAD LITTLE SANDWICH! I MUST FIND SOME MOTHER MALLARD'S MARMALADE TO ADD OR IT WILL BE INEDIBLE!
THERE IS NONE!

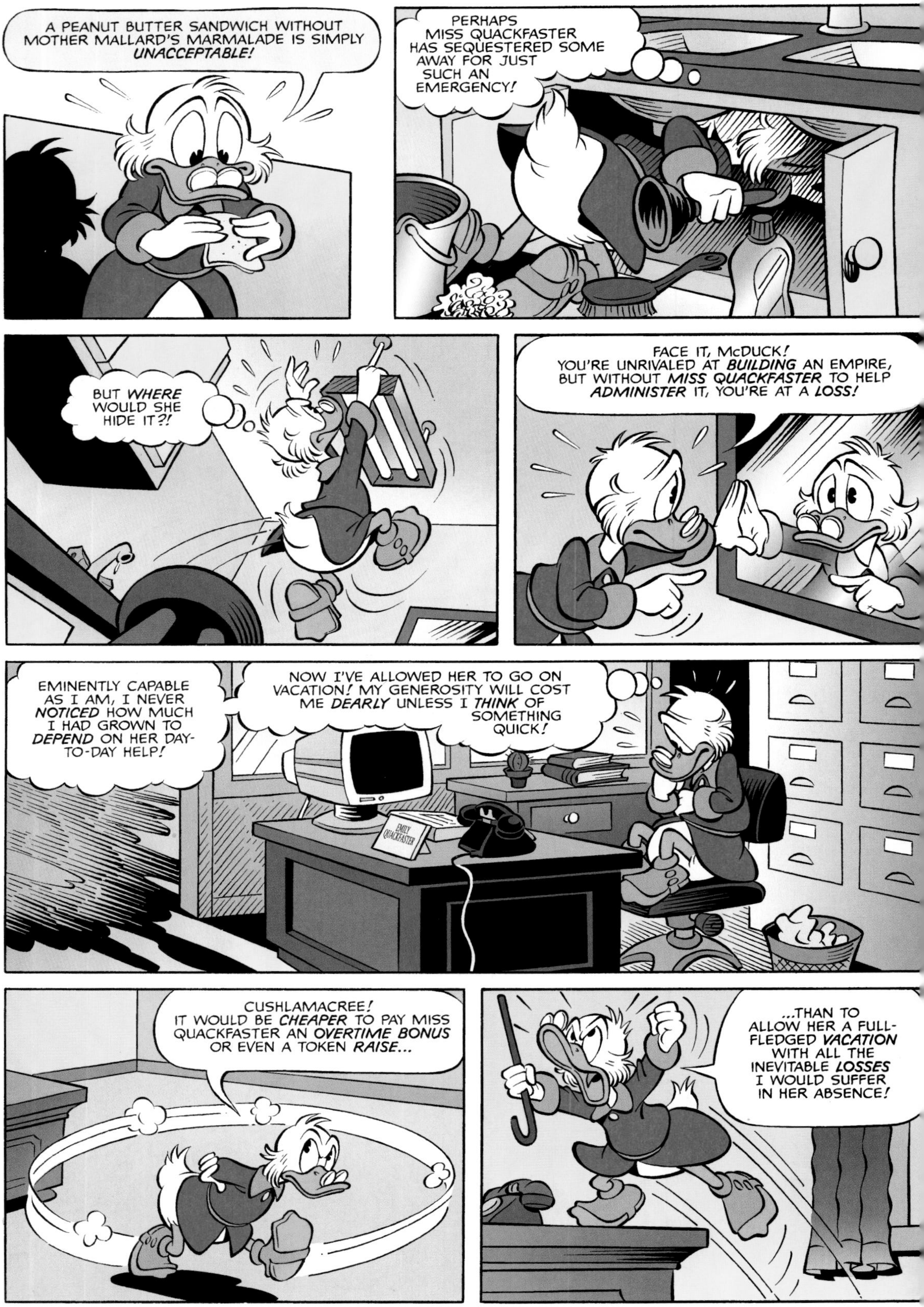
A PEANUT BUTTER SANDWICH WITHOUT MOTHER MALLARD'S MARMALADE IS SIMPLY UNACCEPTABLE!
PERHAPS MISS QUACKFASTER HAS SEQUESTERED SOME AWAY FOR JUST SUCH AN EMERGENCY!
BUT WHERE WOULD SHE HIDE IT?!
FACE IT, McDUCK! YOU'RE UNRIVALED AT BUILDING AN EMPIRE, BUT WITHOUT MISS QUACKFASTER TO HELP ADMINISTER IT, YOU'RE AT A LOSS!
EMINENTLY CAPABLE AS I AM, I NEVER NOTICED HOW MUCH I HAD GROWN TO DEPEND ON HER DAY-TO-DAY HELP!
NOW I'VE ALLOWED HER TO GO ON VACATION! MY GENEROSITY WILL COST ME DEARLY UNLESS I THINK OF SOMETHING QUICK!
EMILY QUACKFASTER
CUSHLAMACREE! IT WOULD BE CHEAPER TO PAY MISS QUACKFASTER AN OVERTIME BONUS OR EVEN A TOKEN RAISE...
...THAN TO ALLOW HER A FULL-FLEDGED VACATION WITH ALL THE INEVITABLE LOSSES I WOULD SUFFER IN HER ABSENCE!

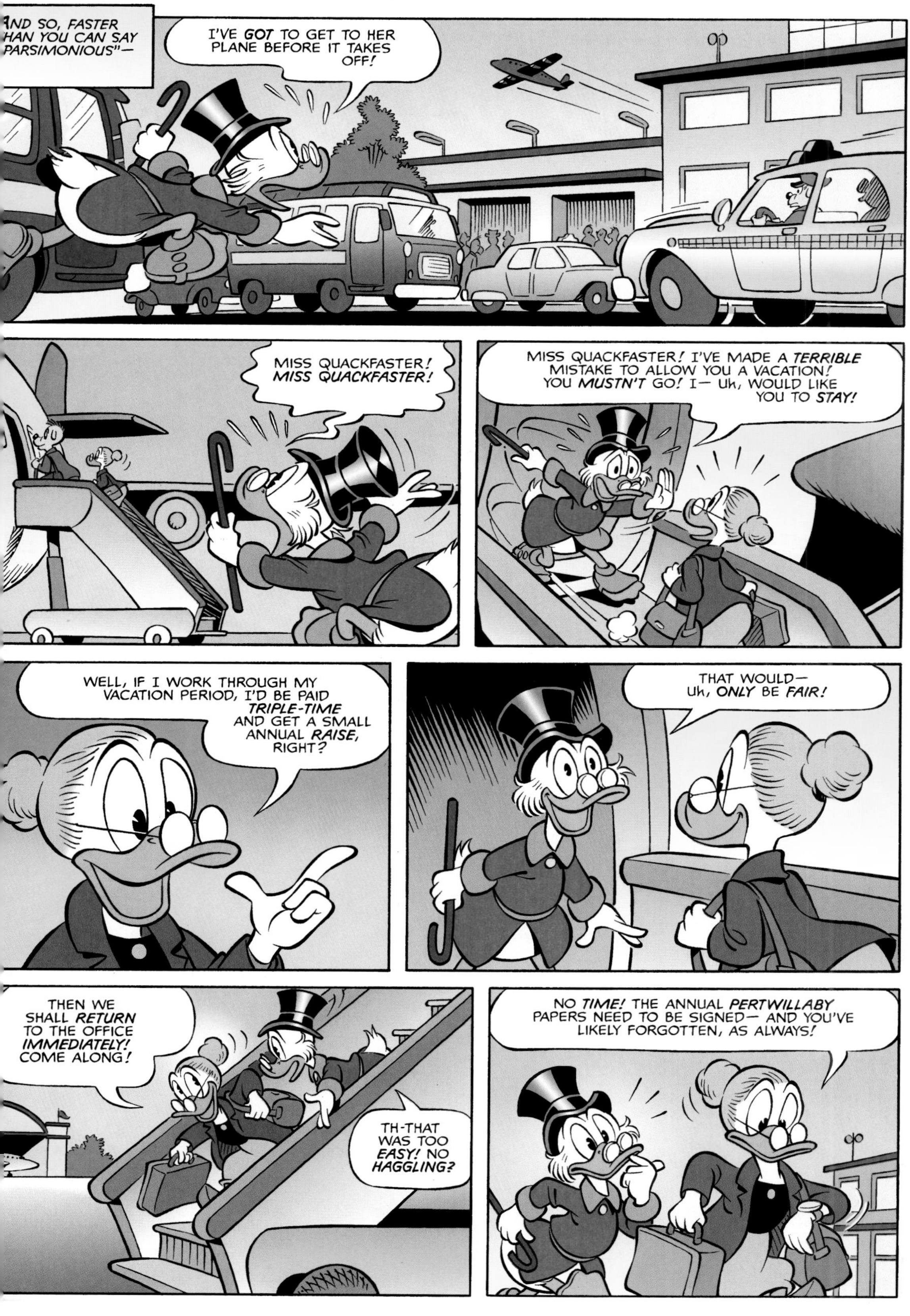
AND SO, FASTER THAN YOU CAN SAY PARSIMONIOUS"—
I'VE GOT TO GET TO HER PLANE BEFORE IT TAKES OFF!
MISS QUACKFASTER! MISS QUACKFASTER!
MISS QUACKFASTER! I'VE MADE A TERRIBLE MISTAKE TO ALLOW YOU A VACATION! YOU MUSTN'T GO! I— Uh, WOULD LIKE YOU TO STAY!
WELL, IF I WORK THROUGH MY VACATION PERIOD, I'D BE PAID TRIPLE-TIME AND GET A SMALL ANNUAL RAISE, RIGHT?
THAT WOULD— Uh, ONLY BE FAIR!
THEN WE SHALL RETURN TO THE OFFICE IMMEDIATELY! COME ALONG!
TH-THAT WAS TOO EASY! NO HAGGLING?
NO TIME! THE ANNUAL PERTWILLABY PAPERS NEED TO BE SIGNED— AND YOU'VE LIKELY FORGOTTEN, AS ALWAYS!

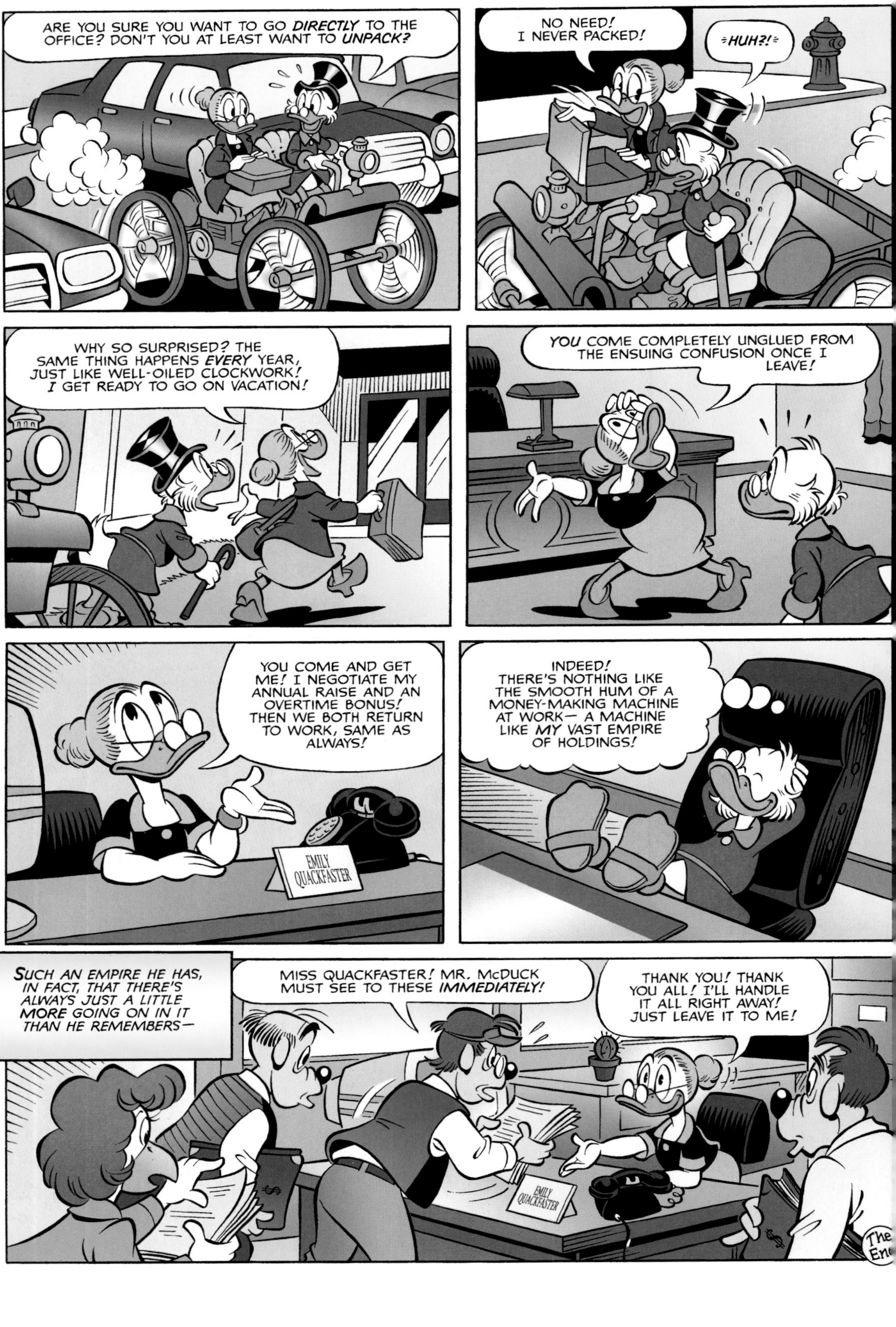
ARE YOU SURE YOU WANT TO GO DIRECTLY TO THE OFFICE? DON'T YOU AT LEAST WANT TO UNPACK?
NO NEED! I NEVER PACKED!
HUH?!
WHY SO SURPRISED? THE SAME THING HAPPENS EVERY YEAR, JUST LIKE WELL-OILED CLOCKWORK! I GET READY TO GO ON VACATION!
YOU COME COMPLETELY UNGLUED FROM THE ENSUING CONFUSION ONCE I LEAVE!
YOU COME AND GET ME! I NEGOTIATE MY ANNUAL RAISE AND AN OVERTIME BONUS! THEN WE BOTH RETURN TO WORK, SAME AS ALWAYS!
EMILY QUACKFASTER
INDEED! THERE'S NOTHING LIKE THE SMOOTH HUM OF A MONEY-MAKING MACHINE AT WORK— A MACHINE LIKE MY VAST EMPIRE OF HOLDINGS!
SUCH AN EMPIRE HE HAS, IN FACT, THAT THERE'S ALWAYS JUST A LITTLE MORE GOING ON IN IT THAN HE REMEMBERS—
MISS QUACKFASTER! MR. McDUCK MUST SEE TO THESE IMMEDIATELY!
THANK YOU! THANK YOU ALL! I'LL HANDLE IT ALL RIGHT AWAY! JUST LEAVE IT TO ME!
EMILY QUACKFASTER

# Walt Disney's GYRO GEARLOOSE in THE GUINEA PIG

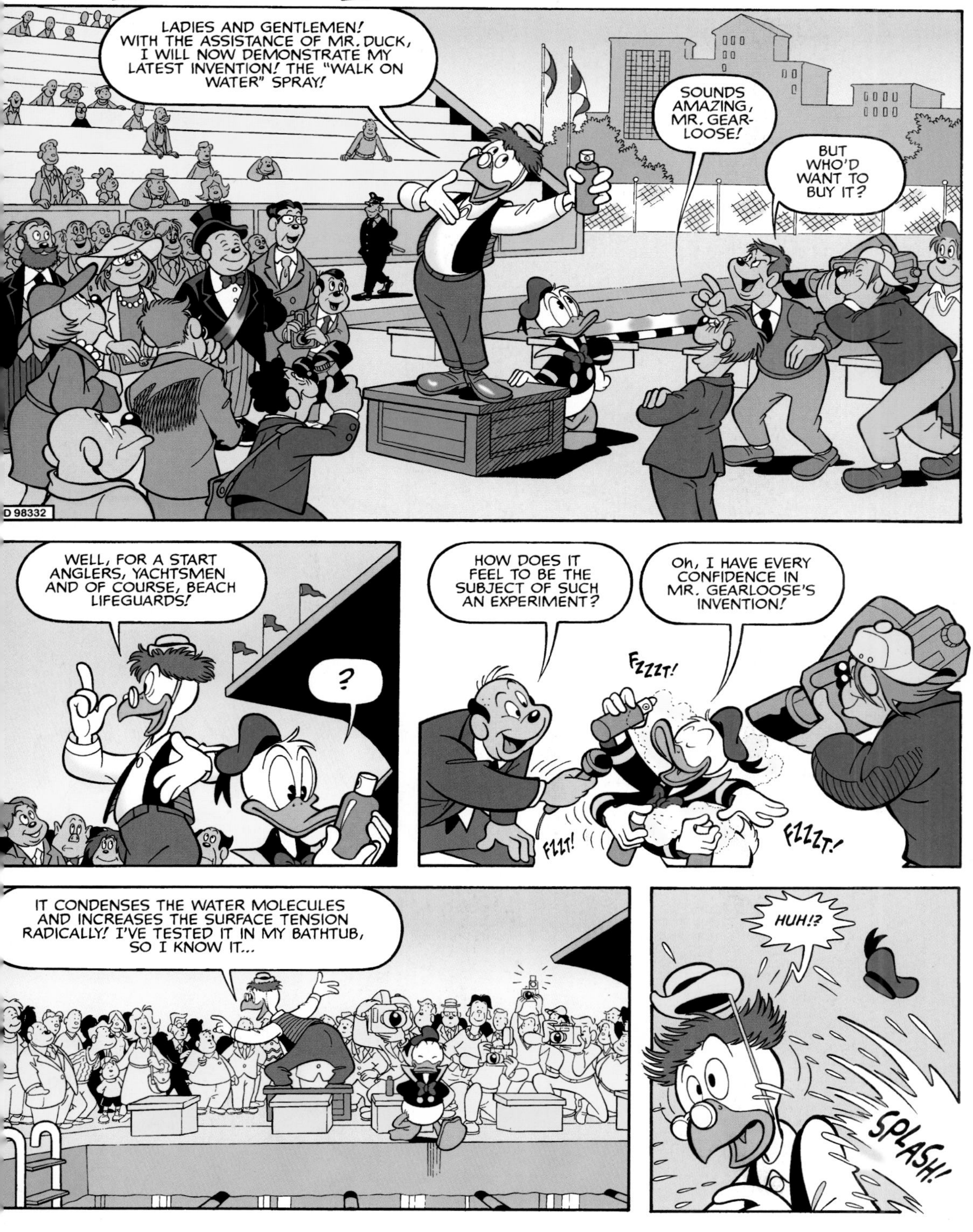
LADIES AND GENTLEMEN! WITH THE ASSISTANCE OF MR. DUCK, I WILL NOW DEMONSTRATE MY LATEST INVENTION! THE "WALK ON WATER" SPRAY!
SOUNDS AMAZING, MR. GEAR-LOOSE!
BUT WHO'D WANT TO BUY IT?
D 98332
WELL, FOR A START ANGLERS, YACHTSMEN AND OF COURSE, BEACH LIFEGUARDS!
?
HOW DOES IT FEEL TO BE THE SUBJECT OF SUCH AN EXPERIMENT?
Oh, I HAVE EVERY CONFIDENCE IN MR. GEARLOOSE'S INVENTION!
FZZZT!
FZZT!
FZZZT!
IT CONDENSES THE WATER MOLECULES AND INCREASES THE SURFACE TENSION RADICALLY! I'VE TESTED IT IN MY BATHTUB, SO I KNOW IT...
HUH!?
SPLASH!

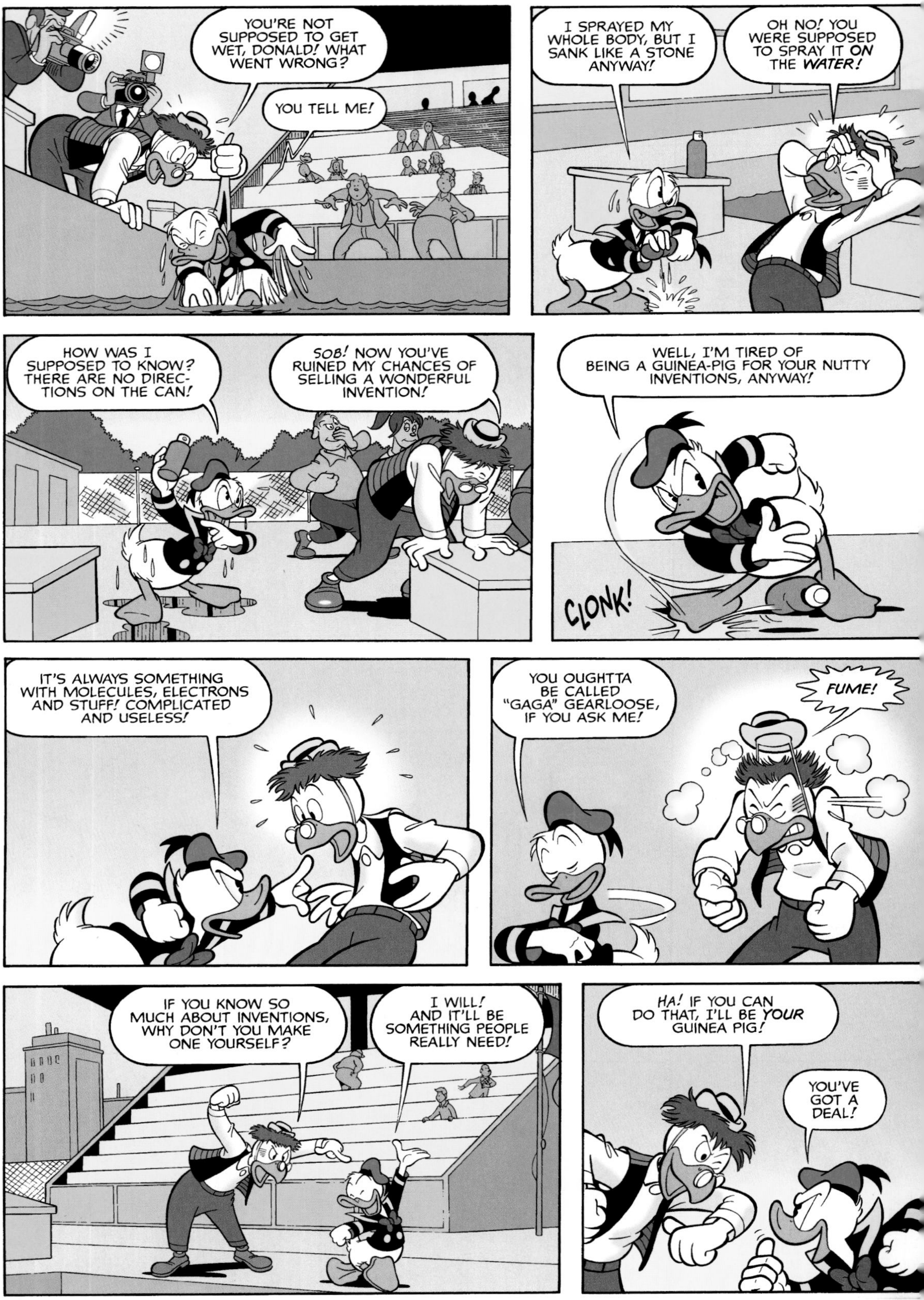
YOU'RE NOT SUPPOSED TO GET WET, DONALD! WHAT WENT WRONG?
YOU TELL ME!
I SPRAYED MY WHOLE BODY, BUT I SANK LIKE A STONE ANYWAY!
OH NO! YOU WERE SUPPOSED TO SPRAY IT ON THE WATER!
HOW WAS I SUPPOSED TO KNOW? THERE ARE NO DIRECTIONS ON THE CAN!
SOB! NOW YOU'VE RUINED MY CHANCES OF SELLING A WONDERFUL INVENTION!
WELL, I'M TIRED OF BEING A GUINEA-PIG FOR YOUR NUTTY INVENTIONS, ANYWAY!
CLONK!
IT'S ALWAYS SOMETHING WITH MOLECULES, ELECTRONS AND STUFF! COMPLICATED AND USELESS!
YOU OUGHTTA BE CALLED "GAGA" GEARLOOSE, IF YOU ASK ME!
FUME!
IF YOU KNOW SO MUCH ABOUT INVENTIONS, WHY DON'T YOU MAKE ONE YOURSELF?
I WILL! AND IT'LL BE SOMETHING PEOPLE REALLY NEED!
HA! IF YOU CAN DO THAT, I'LL BE YOUR GUINEA PIG!
YOU'VE GOT A DEAL!

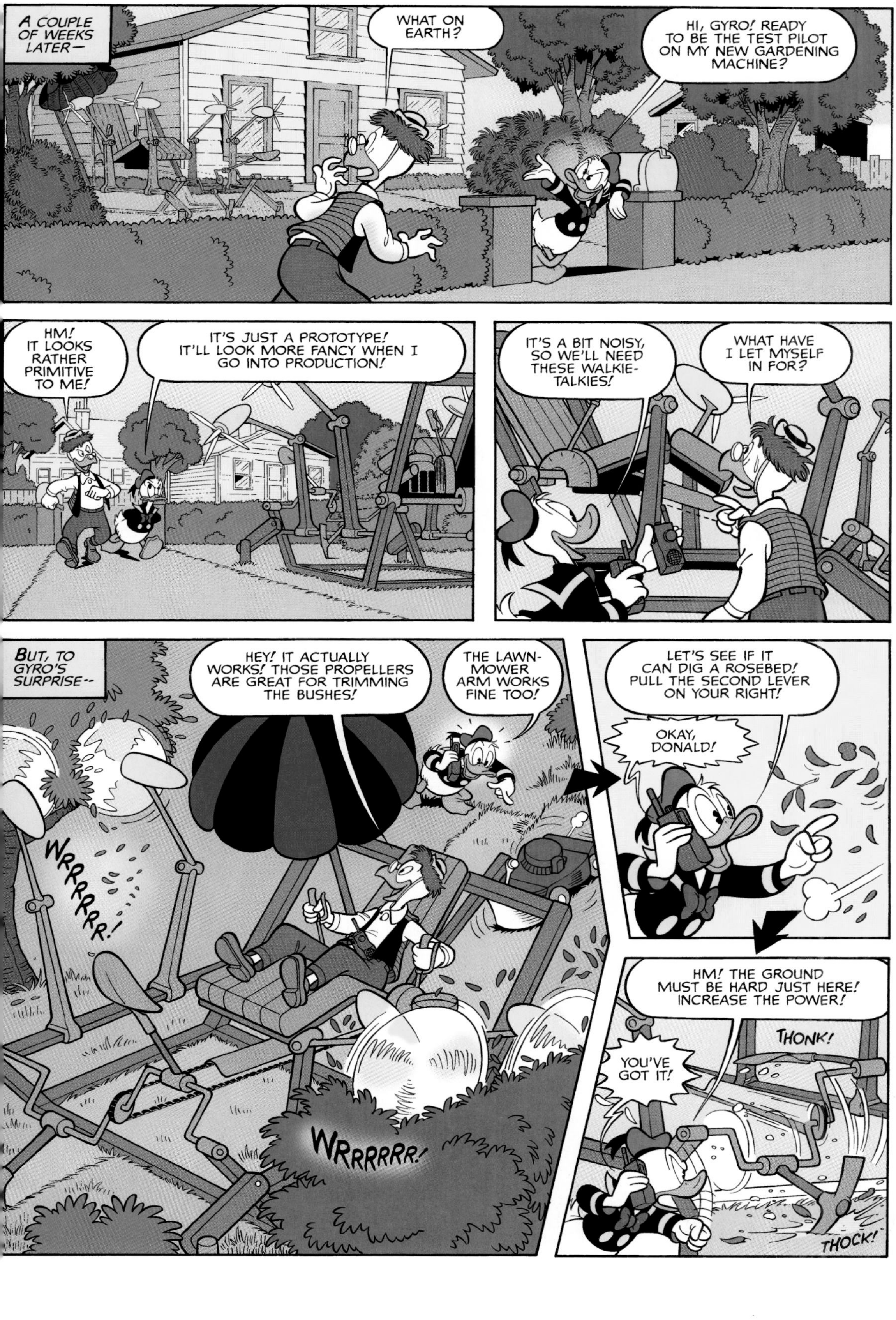
A COUPLE OF WEEKS LATER—
WHAT ON EARTH?
HI, GYRO! READY TO BE THE TEST PILOT ON MY NEW GARDENING MACHINE?
HM! IT LOOKS RATHER PRIMITIVE TO ME!
IT'S JUST A PROTOTYPE! IT'LL LOOK MORE FANCY WHEN I GO INTO PRODUCTION!
IT'S A BIT NOISY, SO WE'LL NEED THESE WALKIE-TALKIES!
WHAT HAVE I LET MYSELF IN FOR?
BUT, TO GYRO'S SURPRISE--
HEY! IT ACTUALLY WORKS! THOSE PROPELLERS ARE GREAT FOR TRIMMING THE BUSHES!
THE LAWN-MOWER ARM WORKS FINE TOO!
WRRRRRR!
WRRRRRR!
LET'S SEE IF IT CAN DIG A ROSEBED! PULL THE SECOND LEVER ON YOUR RIGHT!
OKAY, DONALD!
HM! THE GROUND MUST BE HARD JUST HERE! INCREASE THE POWER!
THONK!
YOU'VE GOT IT!
THOCK!

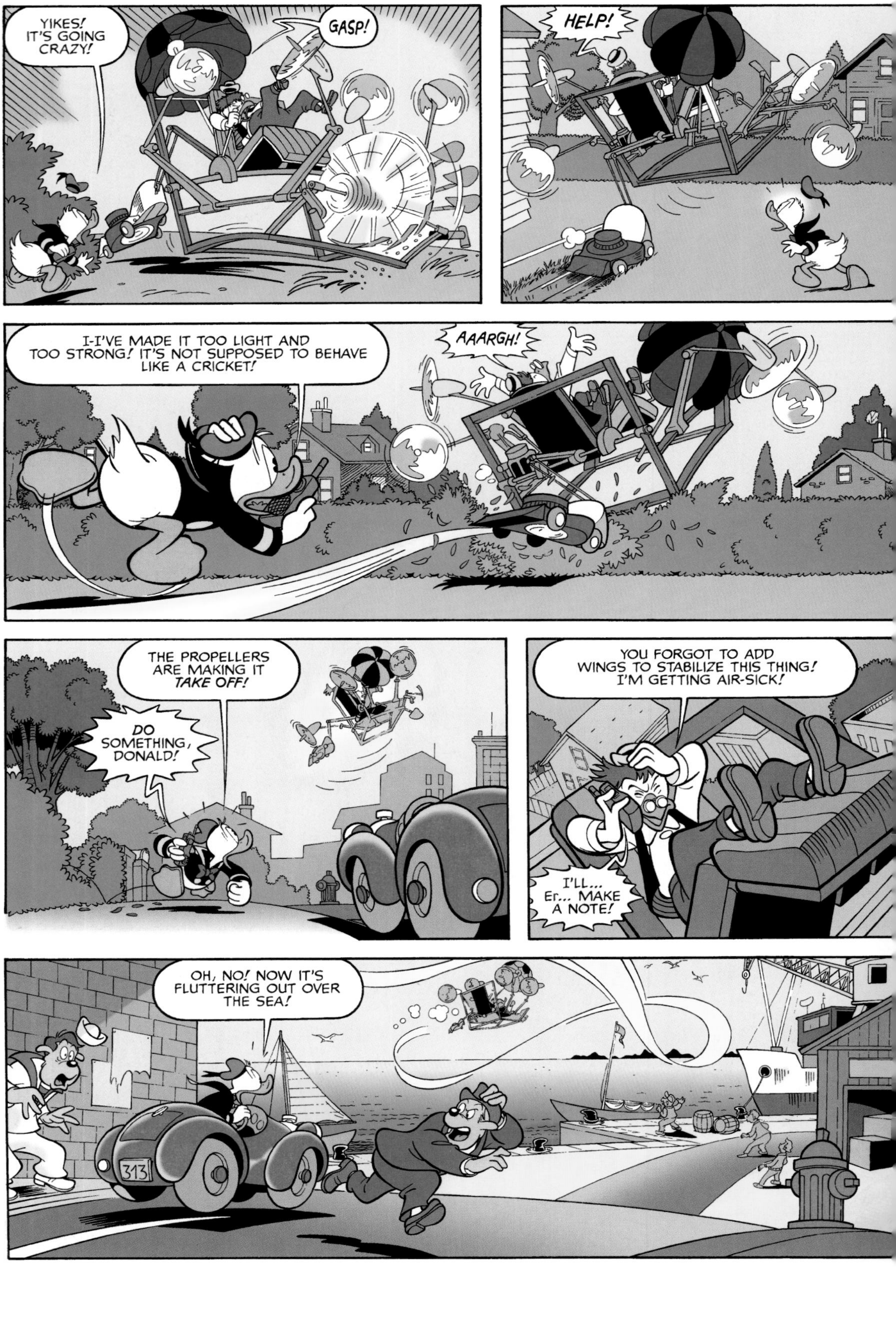
YIKES! IT'S GOING CRAZY!
GASP!
HELP!
I-I'VE MADE IT TOO LIGHT AND TOO STRONG! IT'S NOT SUPPOSED TO BEHAVE LIKE A CRICKET!
AAARGH!
THE PROPELLERS ARE MAKING IT TAKE OFF!
DO SOMETHING, DONALD!
YOU FORGOT TO ADD WINGS TO STABILIZE THIS THING! I'M GETTING AIR-SICK!
I'LL... Er... MAKE A NOTE!
OH, NO! NOW IT'S FLUTTERING OUT OVER THE SEA!
313

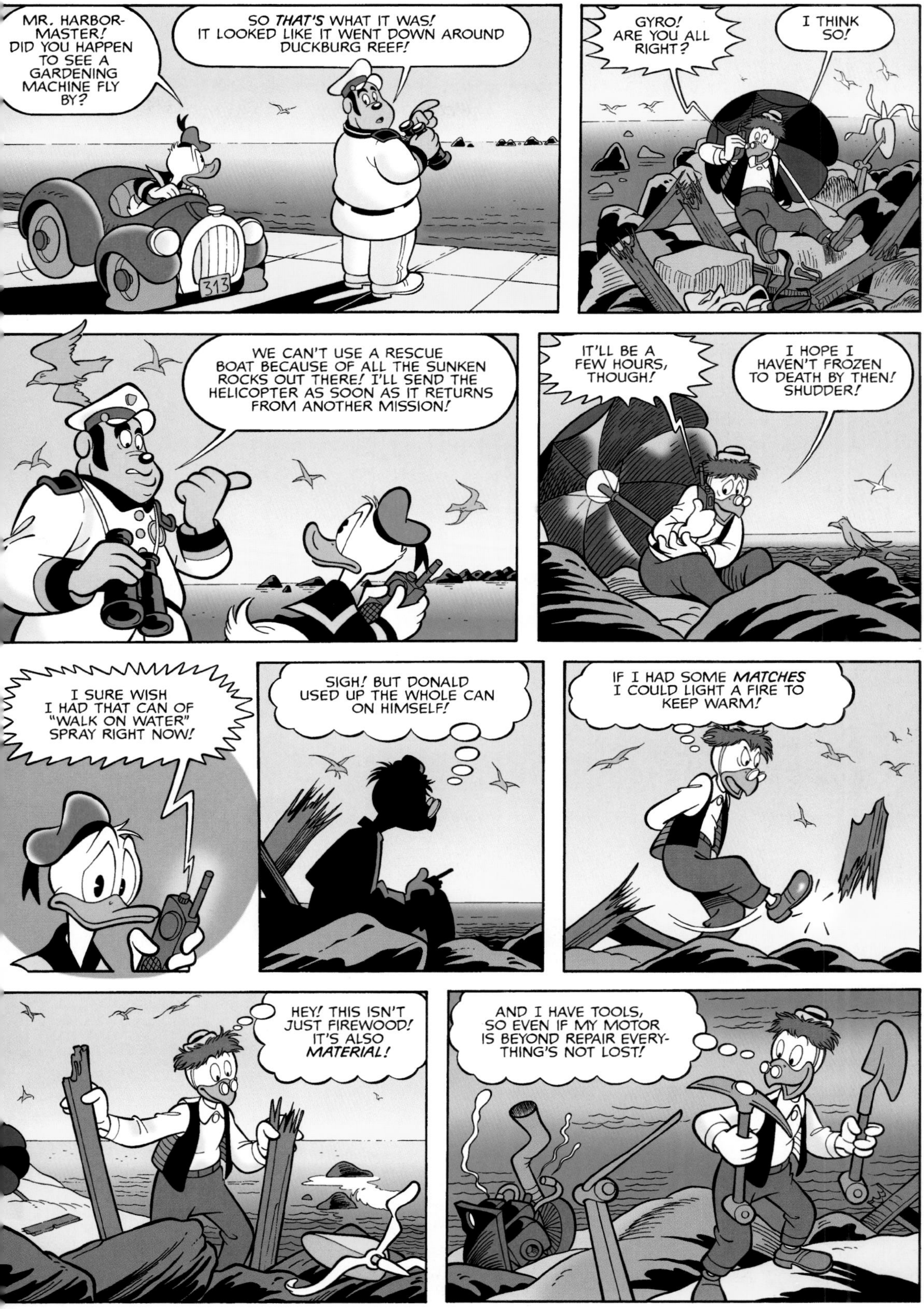
MR. HARBOR-MASTER! DID YOU HAPPEN TO SEE A GARDENING MACHINE FLY BY?
SO THAT'S WHAT IT WAS! IT LOOKED LIKE IT WENT DOWN AROUND DUCKBURG REEF!
313
GYRO! ARE YOU ALL RIGHT?
I THINK SO!
WE CAN'T USE A RESCUE BOAT BECAUSE OF ALL THE SUNKEN ROCKS OUT THERE! I'LL SEND THE HELICOPTER AS SOON AS IT RETURNS FROM ANOTHER MISSION!
IT'LL BE A FEW HOURS, THOUGH!
I HOPE I HAVEN'T FROZEN TO DEATH BY THEN! SHUDDER!
I SURE WISH I HAD THAT CAN OF "WALK ON WATER" SPRAY RIGHT NOW!
SIGH! BUT DONALD USED UP THE WHOLE CAN ON HIMSELF!
IF I HAD SOME MATCHES I COULD LIGHT A FIRE TO KEEP WARM!
HEY! THIS ISN'T JUST FIREWOOD! IT'S ALSO MATERIAL!
AND I HAVE TOOLS, SO EVEN IF MY MOTOR IS BEYOND REPAIR EVERY-THING'S NOT LOST!

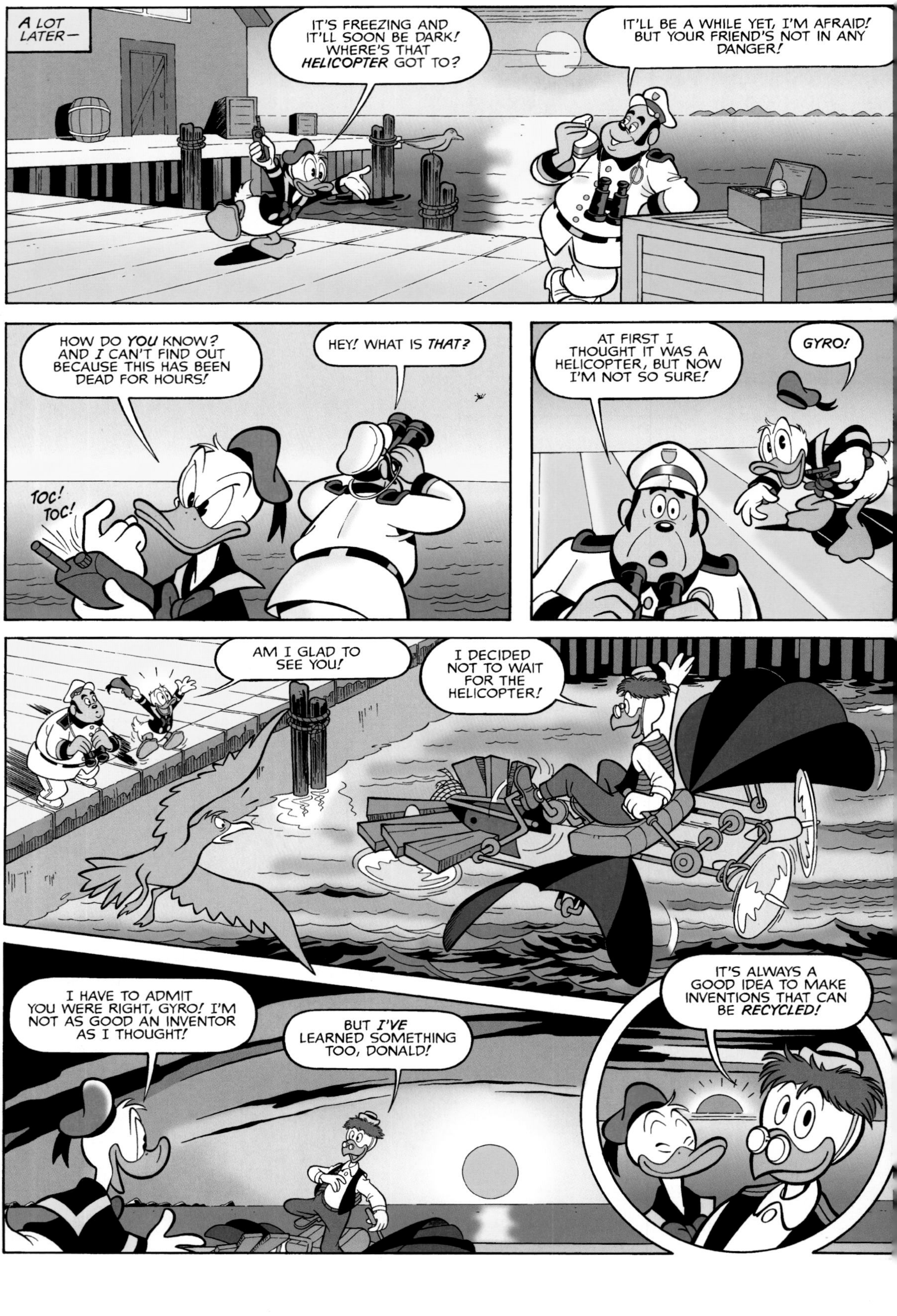
A LOT LATER—
IT'S FREEZING AND IT'LL SOON BE DARK! WHERE'S THAT HELICOPTER GOT TO?
IT'LL BE A WHILE YET, I'M AFRAID! BUT YOUR FRIEND'S NOT IN ANY DANGER!
HOW DO YOU KNOW? AND I CAN'T FIND OUT BECAUSE THIS HAS BEEN DEAD FOR HOURS!
TOC! TOC!
HEY! WHAT IS THAT?
AT FIRST I THOUGHT IT WAS A HELICOPTER, BUT NOW I'M NOT SO SURE!
GYRO!
AM I GLAD TO SEE YOU!
I DECIDED NOT TO WAIT FOR THE HELICOPTER!
I HAVE TO ADMIT YOU WERE RIGHT, GYRO! I'M NOT AS GOOD AN INVENTOR AS I THOUGHT!
BUT I'VE LEARNED SOMETHING TOO, DONALD!
IT'S ALWAYS A GOOD IDEA TO MAKE INVENTIONS THAT CAN BE RECYCLED!

# Walt Disney's Uncle $crooge in Nuts After Nuts Part One

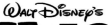

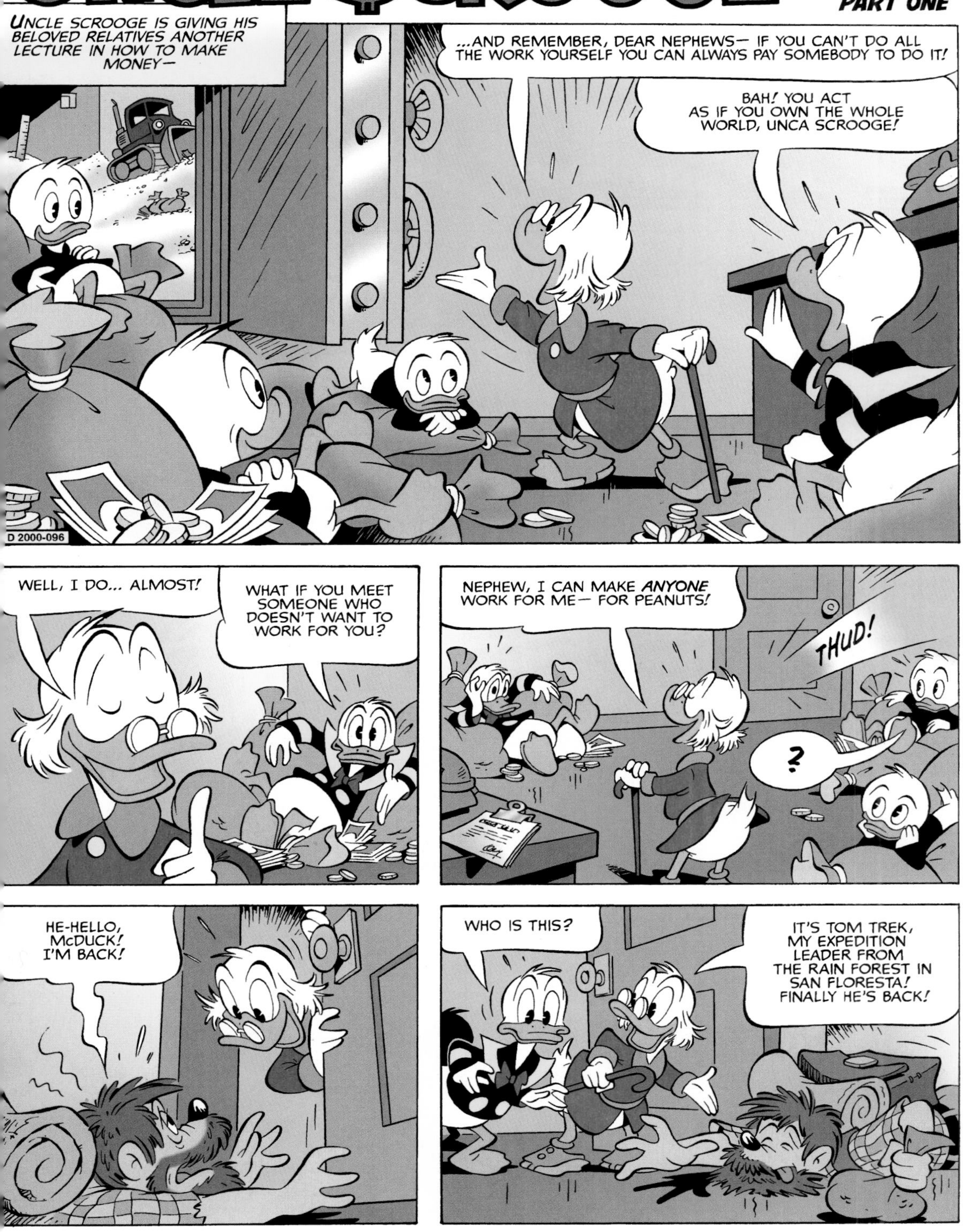
UNCLE SCROOGE IS GIVING HIS BELOVED RELATIVES ANOTHER LECTURE IN HOW TO MAKE MONEY—
...AND REMEMBER, DEAR NEPHEWS— IF YOU CAN'T DO ALL THE WORK YOURSELF YOU CAN ALWAYS PAY SOMEBODY TO DO IT!
BAH! YOU ACT AS IF YOU OWN THE WHOLE WORLD, UNCA SCROOGE!
D 2000-096
WELL, I DO... ALMOST!
WHAT IF YOU MEET SOMEONE WHO DOESN'T WANT TO WORK FOR YOU?
NEPHEW, I CAN MAKE *ANYONE* WORK FOR ME— FOR PEANUTS!
THUD!
?
HE-HELLO, McDUCK! I'M BACK!
WHO IS THIS?
IT'S TOM TREK, MY EXPEDITION LEADER FROM THE RAIN FOREST IN SAN FLORESTA! FINALLY HE'S BACK!

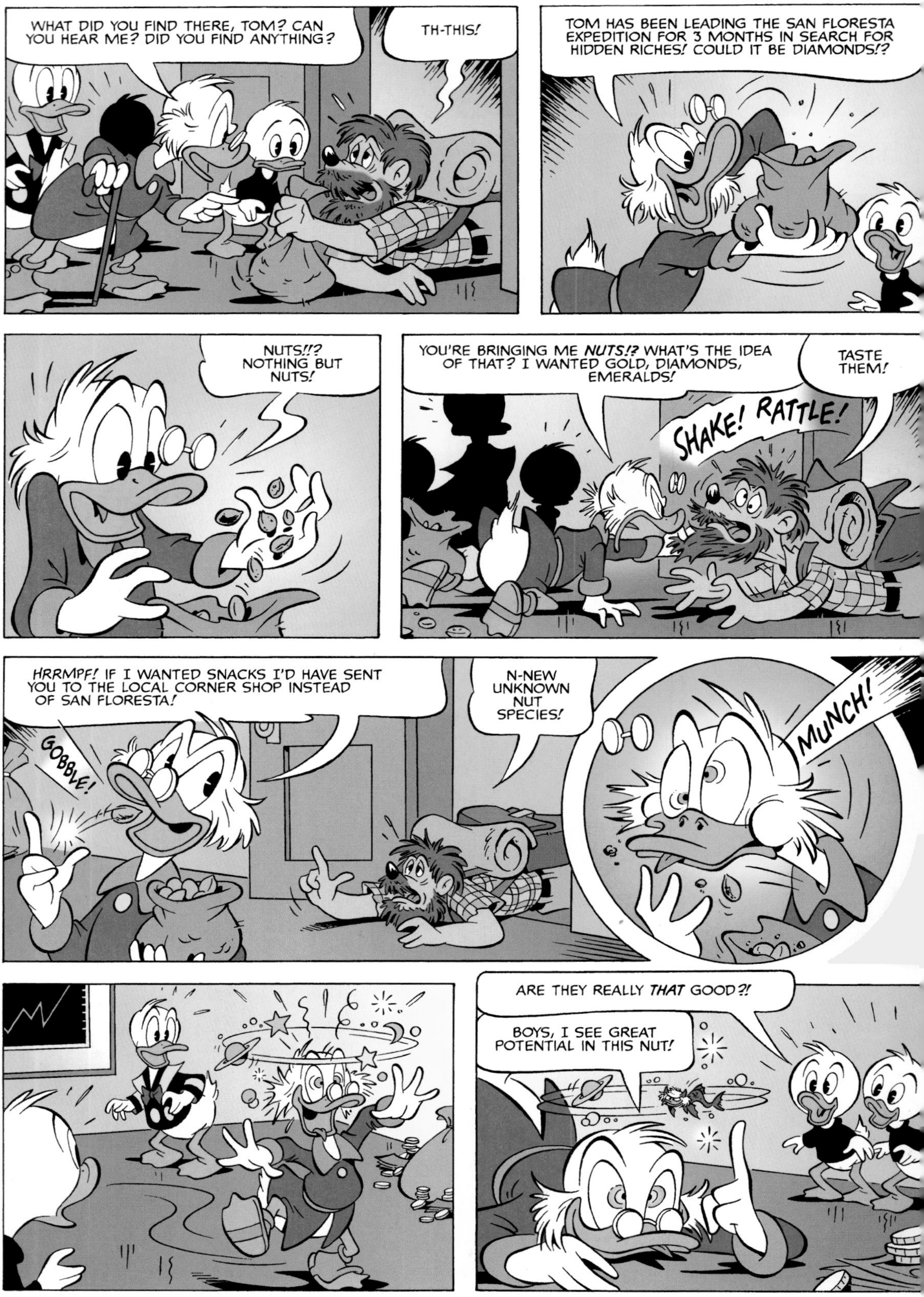
WHAT DID YOU FIND THERE, TOM? CAN YOU HEAR ME? DID YOU FIND ANYTHING?
TH-THIS!
TOM HAS BEEN LEADING THE SAN FLORESTA EXPEDITION FOR 3 MONTHS IN SEARCH FOR HIDDEN RICHES! COULD IT BE DIAMONDS!?
NUTS!!? NOTHING BUT NUTS!
YOU'RE BRINGING ME *NUTS!?* WHAT'S THE IDEA OF THAT? I WANTED GOLD, DIAMONDS, EMERALDS!
TASTE THEM!
SHAKE! RATTLE!
*HRRMPF!* IF I WANTED SNACKS I'D HAVE SENT YOU TO THE LOCAL CORNER SHOP INSTEAD OF SAN FLORESTA!
GOBBLE!
N-NEW UNKNOWN NUT SPECIES!
MUNCH!
ARE THEY REALLY *THAT* GOOD?!
BOYS, I SEE GREAT POTENTIAL IN THIS NUT!

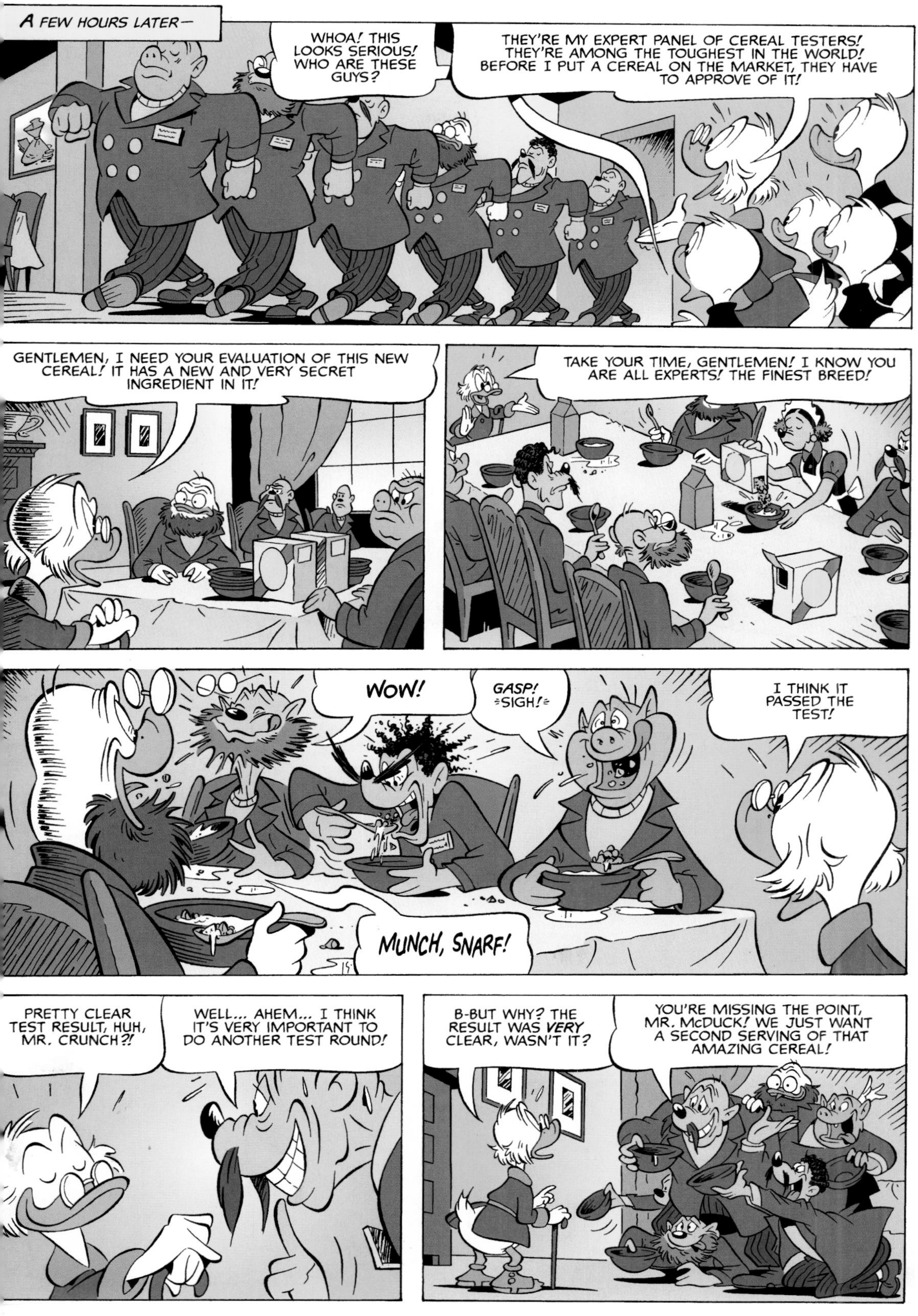
A FEW HOURS LATER—
WHOA! THIS LOOKS SERIOUS! WHO ARE THESE GUYS?
THEY'RE MY EXPERT PANEL OF CEREAL TESTERS! THEY'RE AMONG THE TOUGHEST IN THE WORLD! BEFORE I PUT A CEREAL ON THE MARKET, THEY HAVE TO APPROVE OF IT!
GENTLEMEN, I NEED YOUR EVALUATION OF THIS NEW CEREAL! IT HAS A NEW AND VERY SECRET INGREDIENT IN IT!
TAKE YOUR TIME, GENTLEMEN! I KNOW YOU ARE ALL EXPERTS! THE FINEST BREED!
WOW!
GASP! SIGH!
I THINK IT PASSED THE TEST!
MUNCH, SNARF!
PRETTY CLEAR TEST RESULT, HUH, MR. CRUNCH?!
WELL... AHEM... I THINK IT'S VERY IMPORTANT TO DO ANOTHER TEST ROUND!
B-BUT WHY? THE RESULT WAS VERY CLEAR, WASN'T IT?
YOU'RE MISSING THE POINT, MR. McDUCK! WE JUST WANT A SECOND SERVING OF THAT AMAZING CEREAL!

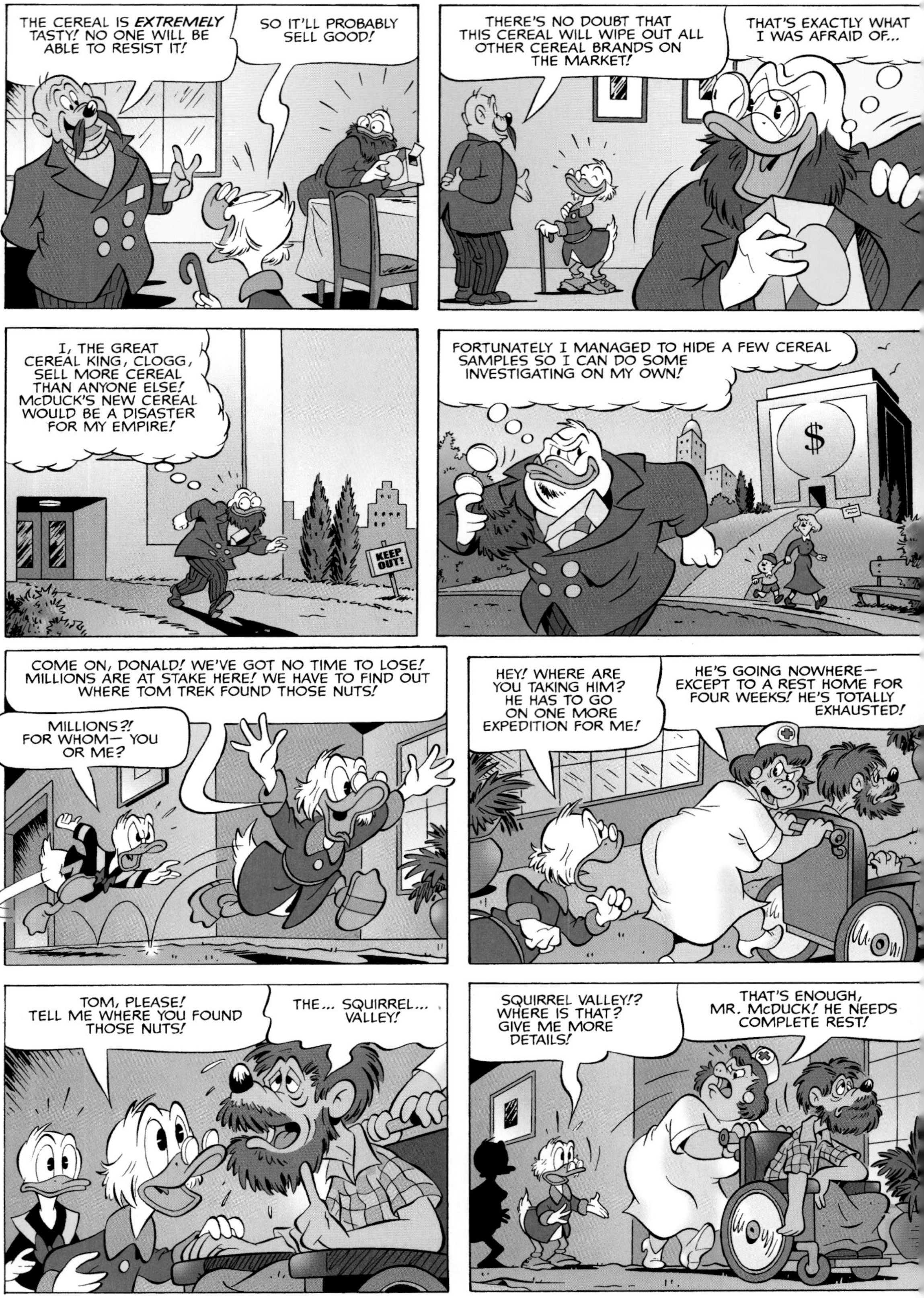
THE CEREAL IS EXTREMELY TASTY! NO ONE WILL BE ABLE TO RESIST IT!
SO IT'LL PROBABLY SELL GOOD!
THERE'S NO DOUBT THAT THIS CEREAL WILL WIPE OUT ALL OTHER CEREAL BRANDS ON THE MARKET!
THAT'S EXACTLY WHAT I WAS AFRAID OF...
I, THE GREAT CEREAL KING, CLOGG, SELL MORE CEREAL THAN ANYONE ELSE! McDUCK'S NEW CEREAL WOULD BE A DISASTER FOR MY EMPIRE!
KEEP OUT!
FORTUNATELY I MANAGED TO HIDE A FEW CEREAL SAMPLES SO I CAN DO SOME INVESTIGATING ON MY OWN!
$
COME ON, DONALD! WE'VE GOT NO TIME TO LOSE! MILLIONS ARE AT STAKE HERE! WE HAVE TO FIND OUT WHERE TOM TREK FOUND THOSE NUTS!
MILLIONS?! FOR WHOM— YOU OR ME?
HEY! WHERE ARE YOU TAKING HIM? HE HAS TO GO ON ONE MORE EXPEDITION FOR ME!
HE'S GOING NOWHERE— EXCEPT TO A REST HOME FOR FOUR WEEKS! HE'S TOTALLY EXHAUSTED!
TOM, PLEASE! TELL ME WHERE YOU FOUND THOSE NUTS!
THE... SQUIRREL... VALLEY!
SQUIRREL VALLEY!? WHERE IS THAT? GIVE ME MORE DETAILS!
THAT'S ENOUGH, MR. McDUCK! HE NEEDS COMPLETE REST!

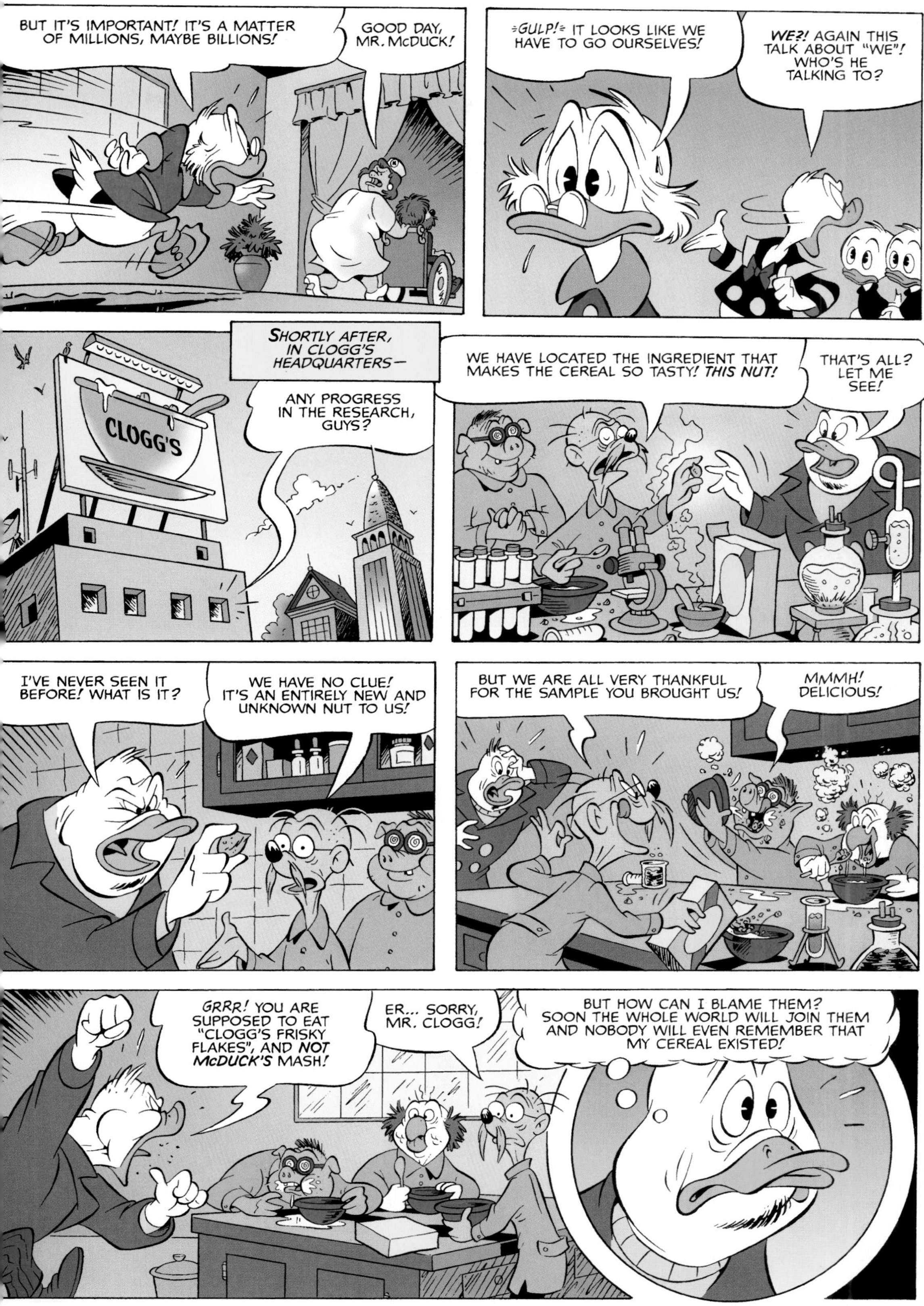
BUT IT'S IMPORTANT! IT'S A MATTER OF MILLIONS, MAYBE BILLIONS!
GOOD DAY, MR. McDUCK!
=GULP!= IT LOOKS LIKE WE HAVE TO GO OURSELVES!
WE?! AGAIN THIS TALK ABOUT "WE"! WHO'S HE TALKING TO?
SHORTLY AFTER, IN CLOGG'S HEADQUARTERS—
CLOGG'S
ANY PROGRESS IN THE RESEARCH, GUYS?
WE HAVE LOCATED THE INGREDIENT THAT MAKES THE CEREAL SO TASTY! THIS NUT!
THAT'S ALL? LET ME SEE!
I'VE NEVER SEEN IT BEFORE! WHAT IS IT?
WE HAVE NO CLUE! IT'S AN ENTIRELY NEW AND UNKNOWN NUT TO US!
BUT WE ARE ALL VERY THANKFUL FOR THE SAMPLE YOU BROUGHT US!
MMMH! DELICIOUS!
GRRR! YOU ARE SUPPOSED TO EAT "CLOGG'S FRISKY FLAKES", AND NOT McDUCK'S MASH!
ER... SORRY, MR. CLOGG!
BUT HOW CAN I BLAME THEM? SOON THE WHOLE WORLD WILL JOIN THEM AND NOBODY WILL EVEN REMEMBER THAT MY CEREAL EXISTED!

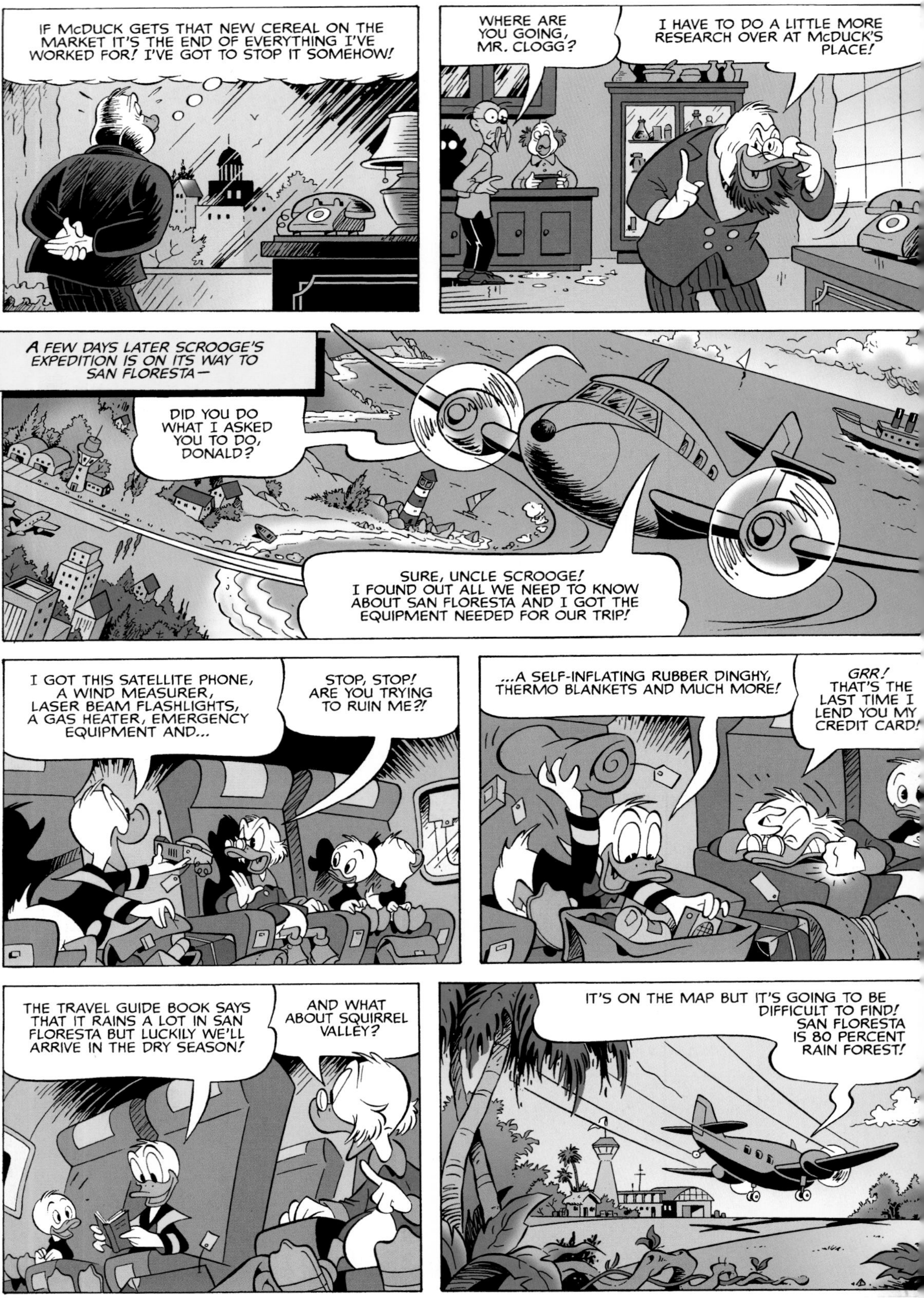

IF McDUCK GETS THAT NEW CEREAL ON THE MARKET IT'S THE END OF EVERYTHING I'VE WORKED FOR! I'VE GOT TO STOP IT SOMEHOW!
WHERE ARE YOU GOING, MR. CLOGG?
I HAVE TO DO A LITTLE MORE RESEARCH OVER AT McDUCK'S PLACE!
A FEW DAYS LATER SCROOGE'S EXPEDITION IS ON ITS WAY TO SAN FLORESTA—
DID YOU DO WHAT I ASKED YOU TO DO, DONALD?
SURE, UNCLE SCROOGE! I FOUND OUT ALL WE NEED TO KNOW ABOUT SAN FLORESTA AND I GOT THE EQUIPMENT NEEDED FOR OUR TRIP!
I GOT THIS SATELLITE PHONE, A WIND MEASURER, LASER BEAM FLASHLIGHTS, A GAS HEATER, EMERGENCY EQUIPMENT AND...
STOP, STOP! ARE YOU TRYING TO RUIN ME?!
...A SELF-INFLATING RUBBER DINGHY, THERMO BLANKETS AND MUCH MORE!
GRR! THAT'S THE LAST TIME I LEND YOU MY CREDIT CARD!
THE TRAVEL GUIDE BOOK SAYS THAT IT RAINS A LOT IN SAN FLORESTA BUT LUCKILY WE'LL ARRIVE IN THE DRY SEASON!
AND WHAT ABOUT SQUIRREL VALLEY?
IT'S ON THE MAP BUT IT'S GOING TO BE DIFFICULT TO FIND! SAN FLORESTA IS 80 PERCENT RAIN FOREST!

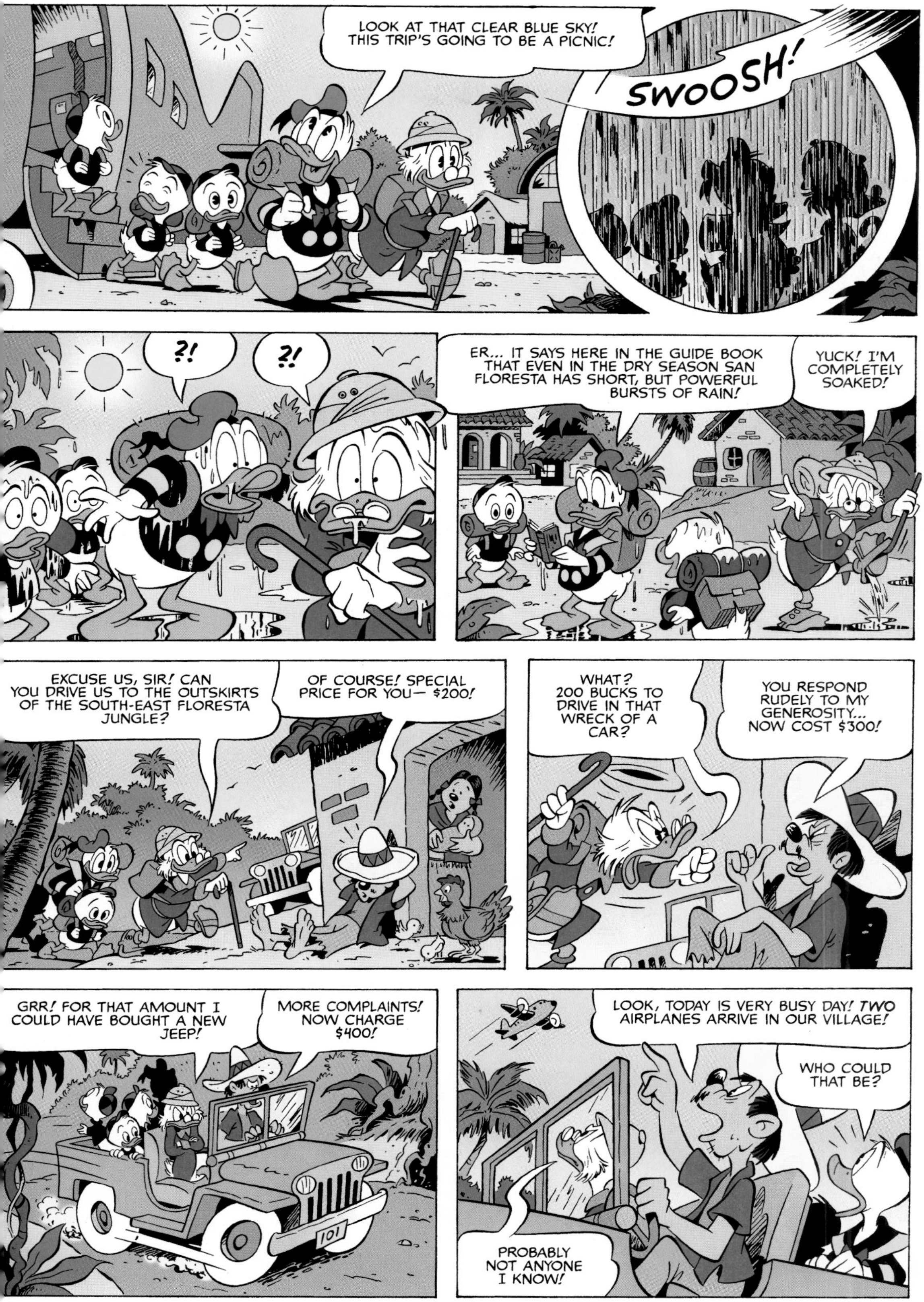
LOOK AT THAT CLEAR BLUE SKY! THIS TRIP'S GOING TO BE A PICNIC!
SWOOSH!
?!
?!
ER... IT SAYS HERE IN THE GUIDE BOOK THAT EVEN IN THE DRY SEASON SAN FLORESTA HAS SHORT, BUT POWERFUL BURSTS OF RAIN!
YUCK! I'M COMPLETELY SOAKED!
EXCUSE US, SIR! CAN YOU DRIVE US TO THE OUTSKIRTS OF THE SOUTH-EAST FLORESTA JUNGLE?
OF COURSE! SPECIAL PRICE FOR YOU— $200!
WHAT? 200 BUCKS TO DRIVE IN THAT WRECK OF A CAR?
YOU RESPOND RUDELY TO MY GENEROSITY... NOW COST $300!
GRR! FOR THAT AMOUNT I COULD HAVE BOUGHT A NEW JEEP!
MORE COMPLAINTS! NOW CHARGE $400!
101
LOOK, TODAY IS VERY BUSY DAY! TWO AIRPLANES ARRIVE IN OUR VILLAGE!
WHO COULD THAT BE?
PROBABLY NOT ANYONE I KNOW!

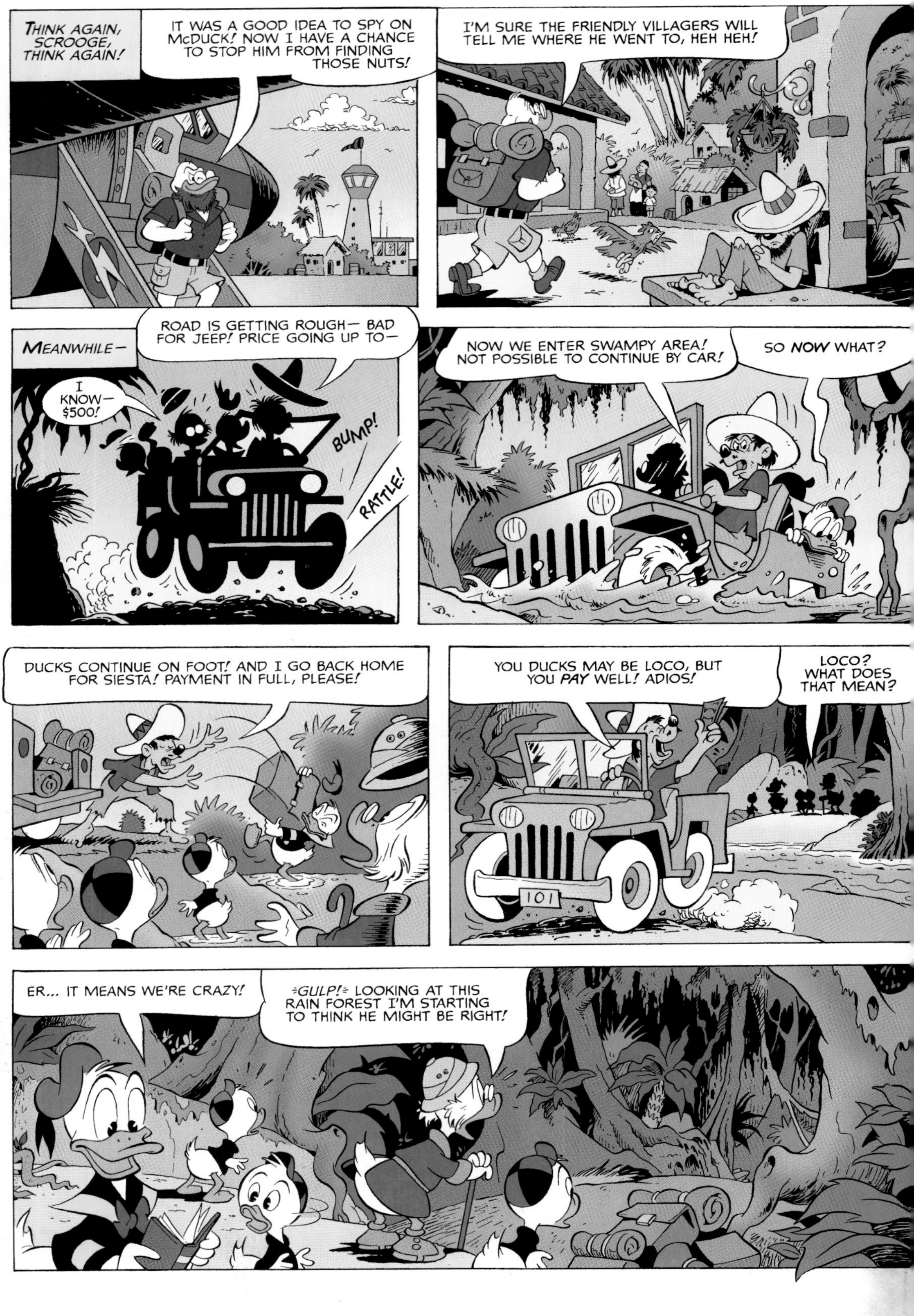
THINK AGAIN, SCROOGE, THINK AGAIN!
IT WAS A GOOD IDEA TO SPY ON McDUCK! NOW I HAVE A CHANCE TO STOP HIM FROM FINDING THOSE NUTS!
I'M SURE THE FRIENDLY VILLAGERS WILL TELL ME WHERE HE WENT TO, HEH HEH!
MEANWHILE—
ROAD IS GETTING ROUGH— BAD FOR JEEP! PRICE GOING UP TO—
I KNOW— $500!
BUMP!
RATTLE!
NOW WE ENTER SWAMPY AREA! NOT POSSIBLE TO CONTINUE BY CAR!
SO NOW WHAT?
DUCKS CONTINUE ON FOOT! AND I GO BACK HOME FOR SIESTA! PAYMENT IN FULL, PLEASE!
YOU DUCKS MAY BE LOCO, BUT YOU PAY WELL! ADIOS!
LOCO? WHAT DOES THAT MEAN?
101
ER... IT MEANS WE'RE CRAZY!
=GULP!= LOOKING AT THIS RAIN FOREST I'M STARTING TO THINK HE MIGHT BE RIGHT!

# How much is your collection worth?

All characters ©2003 respective Copyright holders. All rights reserved.

©2003 Disney Enterprises, Inc.

## Find out with the Definitive Visual Guide and Checklist!™

This edition includes more than 13,000 photo illustrated entries and more than 39,000 prices in 360 unique categories! It's all in here! Toy Story, Uncle Scrooge, Spider-Man, Superman, Small Soldiers, Superhero Resins, Batman, Muhammad Ali, Disneyana, Roy Rogers, Buck Rogers, KISS, Mickey Mouse, The Lone Ranger, Puppet Master, Elvis, The Phantom, X-Men, Charlie Chaplin, The Cisco Kid, Donald Duck, Captain Marvel, Laurel & Hardy, Howdy Doody, Planet of the Apes, MAD, Hopalong Cassidy, Captain America, Toy Guns and more!

**$35** (+s&h)

Available at your local comic book shop. Can't find a comic shop near you? Try the Toll Free Comic Shop Locator Service at (888) COMIC BOOK. Or you can order direct from Gemstone Publishing by calling Toll Free (888) 375-9800 ext. 249.

COMIC SHOP LOCATOR SERVICE
888-COMIC-BOOK
888-266-4226

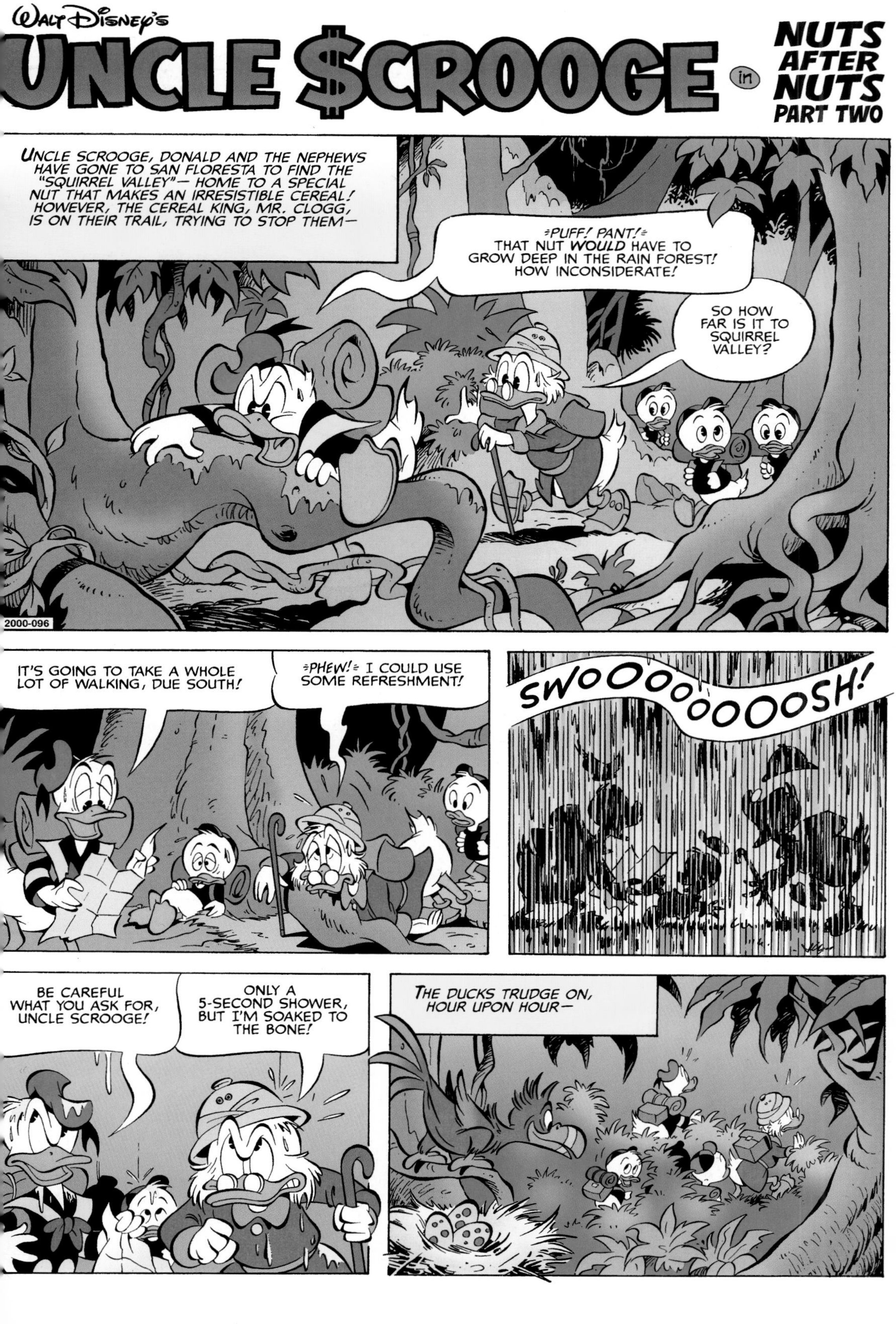
WALT DISNEY'S
UNCLE $CROOGE in
NUTS AFTER NUTS
PART TWO
UNCLE SCROOGE, DONALD AND THE NEPHEWS HAVE GONE TO SAN FLORESTA TO FIND THE "SQUIRREL VALLEY"— HOME TO A SPECIAL NUT THAT MAKES AN IRRESISTIBLE CEREAL! HOWEVER, THE CEREAL KING, MR. CLOGG, IS ON THEIR TRAIL, TRYING TO STOP THEM—
=PUFF! PANT!= THAT NUT WOULD HAVE TO GROW DEEP IN THE RAIN FOREST! HOW INCONSIDERATE!
SO HOW FAR IS IT TO SQUIRREL VALLEY?
2000-096
IT'S GOING TO TAKE A WHOLE LOT OF WALKING, DUE SOUTH!
=PHEW!= I COULD USE SOME REFRESHMENT!
SWOOOOOOOOOSH!
BE CAREFUL WHAT YOU ASK FOR, UNCLE SCROOGE!
ONLY A 5-SECOND SHOWER, BUT I'M SOAKED TO THE BONE!
THE DUCKS TRUDGE ON, HOUR UPON HOUR—

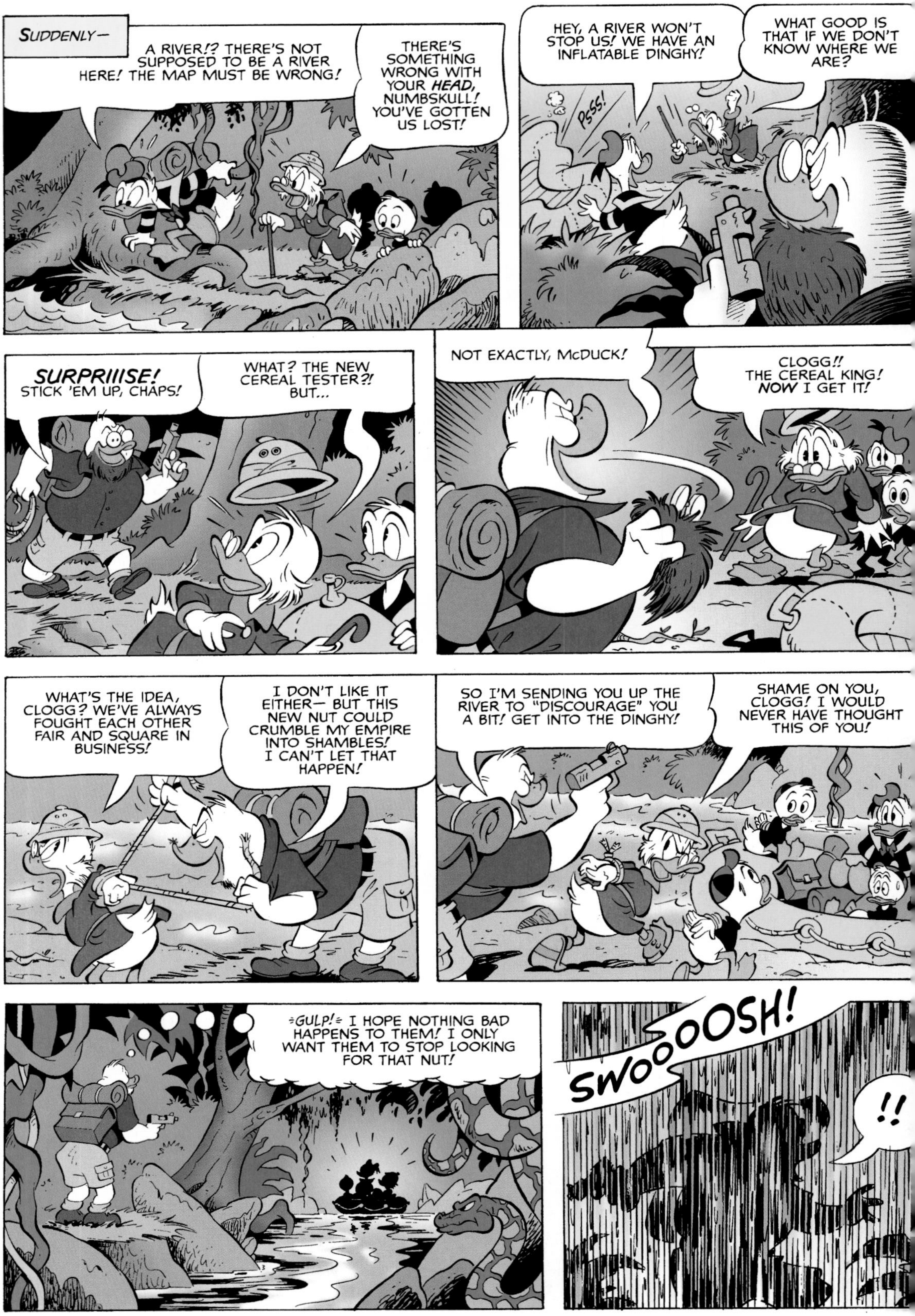
SUDDENLY—
A RIVER!? THERE'S NOT SUPPOSED TO BE A RIVER HERE! THE MAP MUST BE WRONG!
THERE'S SOMETHING WRONG WITH YOUR HEAD, NUMBSKULL! YOU'VE GOTTEN US LOST!
HEY, A RIVER WON'T STOP US! WE HAVE AN INFLATABLE DINGHY!
PSSS!
WHAT GOOD IS THAT IF WE DON'T KNOW WHERE WE ARE?
SURPRIIISE! STICK 'EM UP, CHAPS!
WHAT? THE NEW CEREAL TESTER?! BUT...
NOT EXACTLY, McDUCK!
CLOGG!! THE CEREAL KING! NOW I GET IT!
WHAT'S THE IDEA, CLOGG? WE'VE ALWAYS FOUGHT EACH OTHER FAIR AND SQUARE IN BUSINESS!
I DON'T LIKE IT EITHER— BUT THIS NEW NUT COULD CRUMBLE MY EMPIRE INTO SHAMBLES! I CAN'T LET THAT HAPPEN!
SO I'M SENDING YOU UP THE RIVER TO "DISCOURAGE" YOU A BIT! GET INTO THE DINGHY!
SHAME ON YOU, CLOGG! I WOULD NEVER HAVE THOUGHT THIS OF YOU!
GULP! I HOPE NOTHING BAD HAPPENS TO THEM! I ONLY WANT THEM TO STOP LOOKING FOR THAT NUT!
SWOOOOOSH!
!!

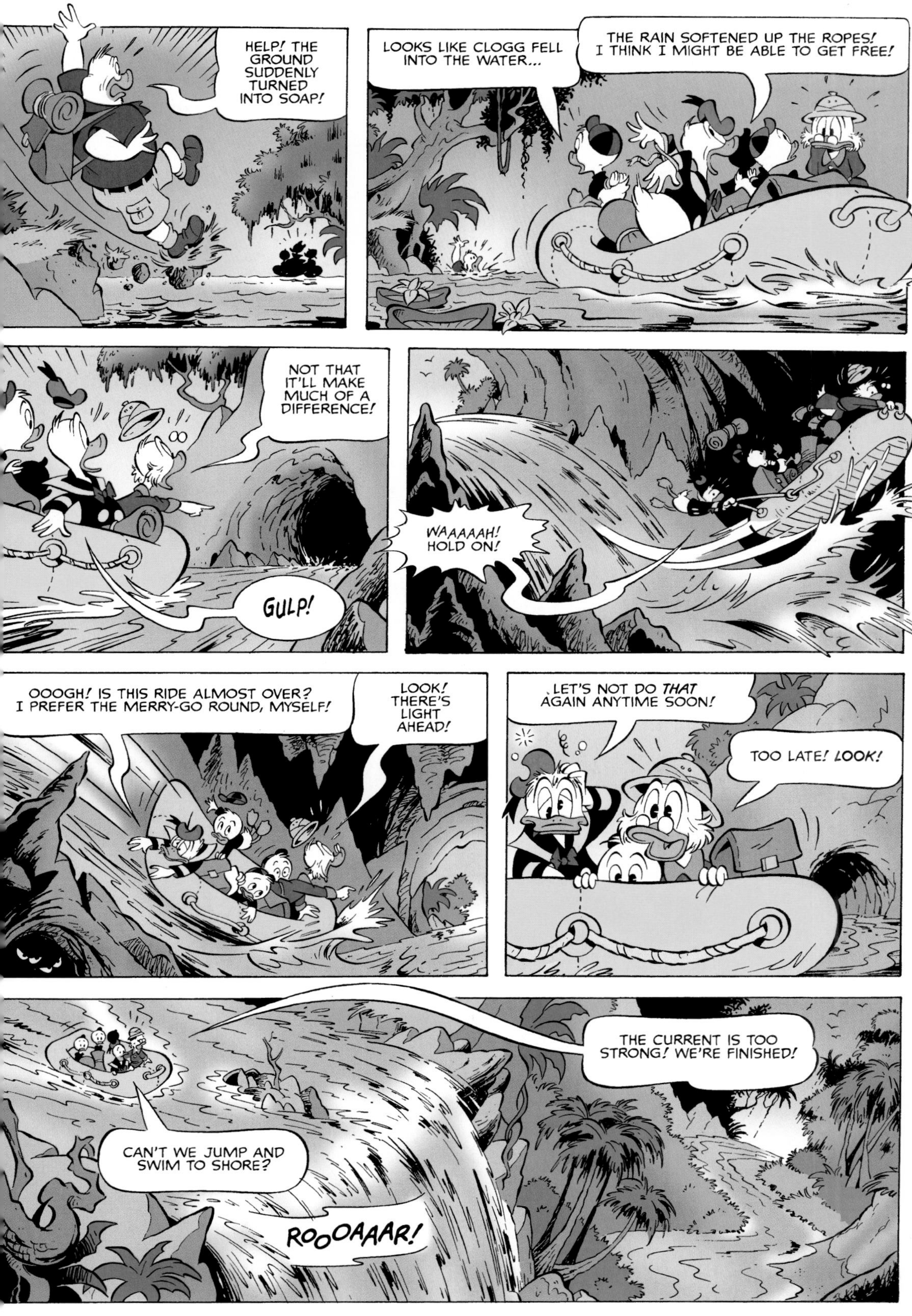
HELP! THE GROUND SUDDENLY TURNED INTO SOAP!
LOOKS LIKE CLOGG FELL INTO THE WATER...
THE RAIN SOFTENED UP THE ROPES! I THINK I MIGHT BE ABLE TO GET FREE!
NOT THAT IT'LL MAKE MUCH OF A DIFFERENCE!
GULP!
WAAAAAH! HOLD ON!
OOOGH! IS THIS RIDE ALMOST OVER? I PREFER THE MERRY-GO ROUND, MYSELF!
LOOK! THERE'S LIGHT AHEAD!
LET'S NOT DO THAT AGAIN ANYTIME SOON!
TOO LATE! LOOK!
THE CURRENT IS TOO STRONG! WE'RE FINISHED!
CAN'T WE JUMP AND SWIM TO SHORE?
ROOOAAAR!

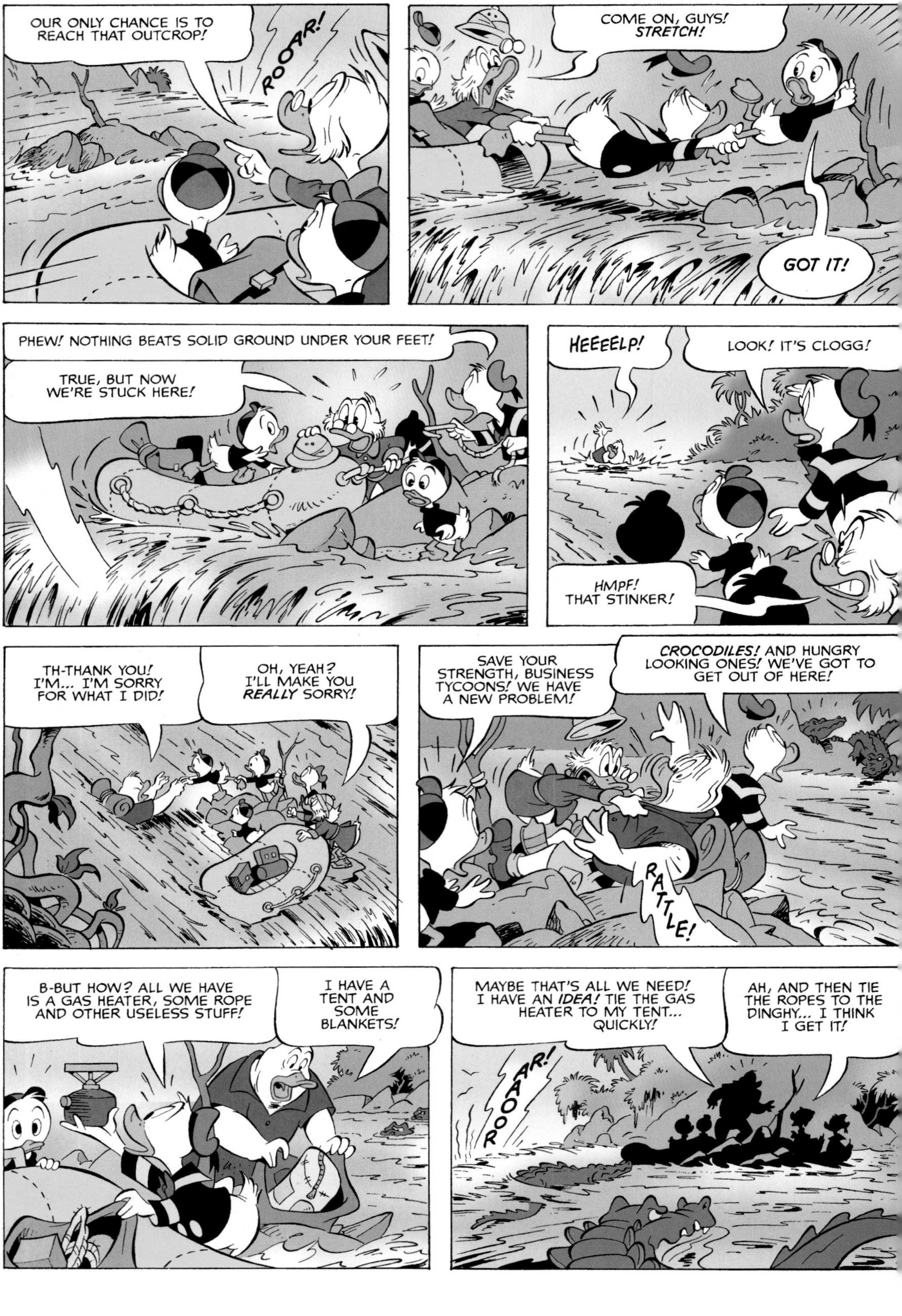
OUR ONLY CHANCE IS TO REACH THAT OUTCROP!
ROOAR!
COME ON, GUYS! STRETCH!
GOT IT!
PHEW! NOTHING BEATS SOLID GROUND UNDER YOUR FEET!
TRUE, BUT NOW WE'RE STUCK HERE!
HEEEELP!
LOOK! IT'S CLOGG!
HMPF! THAT STINKER!
TH-THANK YOU! I'M... I'M SORRY FOR WHAT I DID!
OH, YEAH? I'LL MAKE YOU REALLY SORRY!
SAVE YOUR STRENGTH, BUSINESS TYCOONS! WE HAVE A NEW PROBLEM!
CROCODILES! AND HUNGRY LOOKING ONES! WE'VE GOT TO GET OUT OF HERE!
RATTLE!
B-BUT HOW? ALL WE HAVE IS A GAS HEATER, SOME ROPE AND OTHER USELESS STUFF!
I HAVE A TENT AND SOME BLANKETS!
MAYBE THAT'S ALL WE NEED! I HAVE AN IDEA! TIE THE GAS HEATER TO MY TENT... QUICKLY!
AH, AND THEN TIE THE ROPES TO THE DINGHY... I THINK I GET IT!
ROOOAAR!

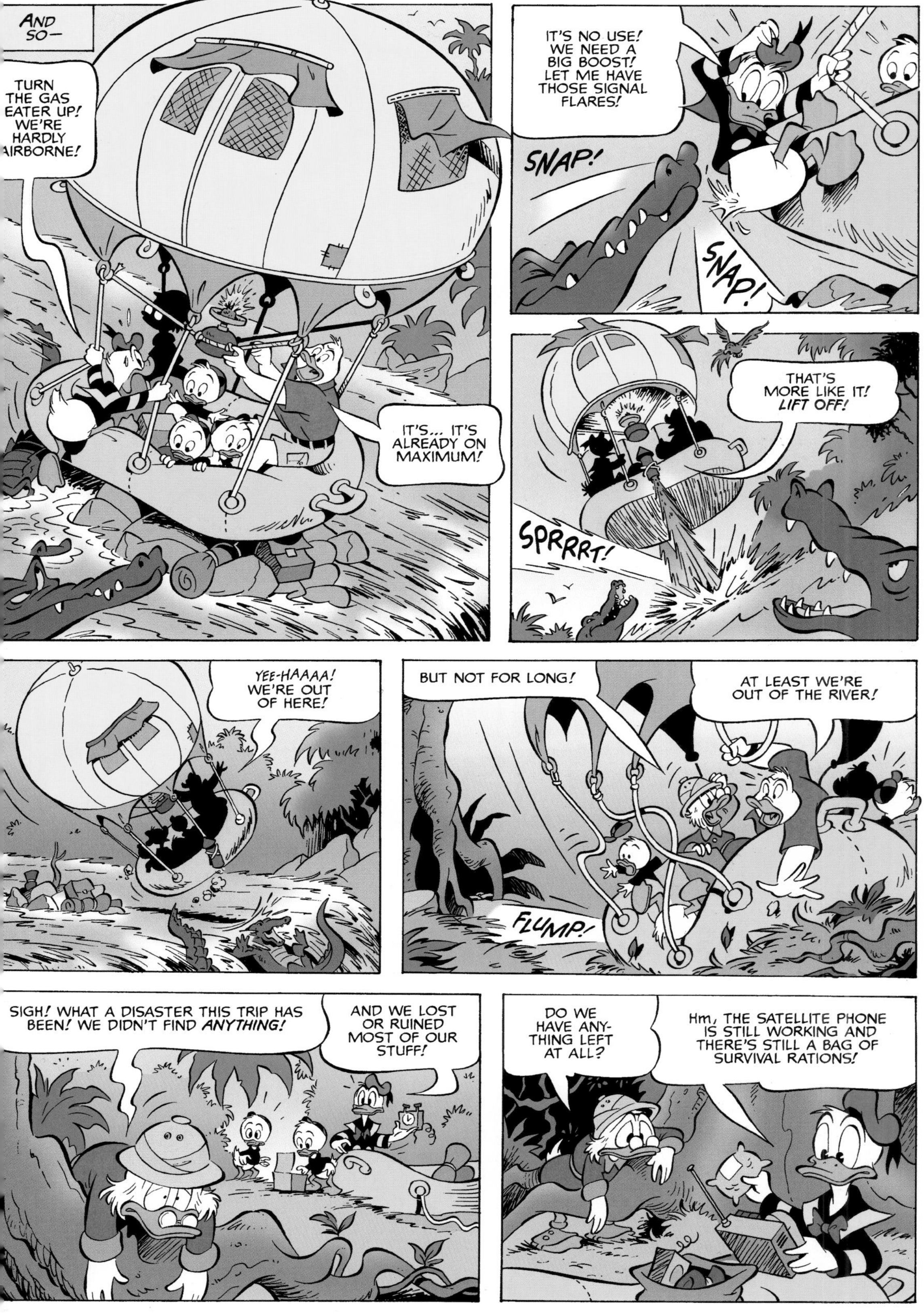
AND SO—
TURN THE GAS EATER UP! WE'RE HARDLY AIRBORNE!
IT'S... IT'S ALREADY ON MAXIMUM!
IT'S NO USE! WE NEED A BIG BOOST! LET ME HAVE THOSE SIGNAL FLARES!
SNAP!
SNAP!
THAT'S MORE LIKE IT! LIFT OFF!
SPRRRT!
YEE-HAAAA! WE'RE OUT OF HERE!
BUT NOT FOR LONG!
AT LEAST WE'RE OUT OF THE RIVER!
FLUMP!
SIGH! WHAT A DISASTER THIS TRIP HAS BEEN! WE DIDN'T FIND ANYTHING!
AND WE LOST OR RUINED MOST OF OUR STUFF!
DO WE HAVE ANYTHING LEFT AT ALL?
Hm, THE SATELLITE PHONE IS STILL WORKING AND THERE'S STILL A BAG OF SURVIVAL RATIONS!

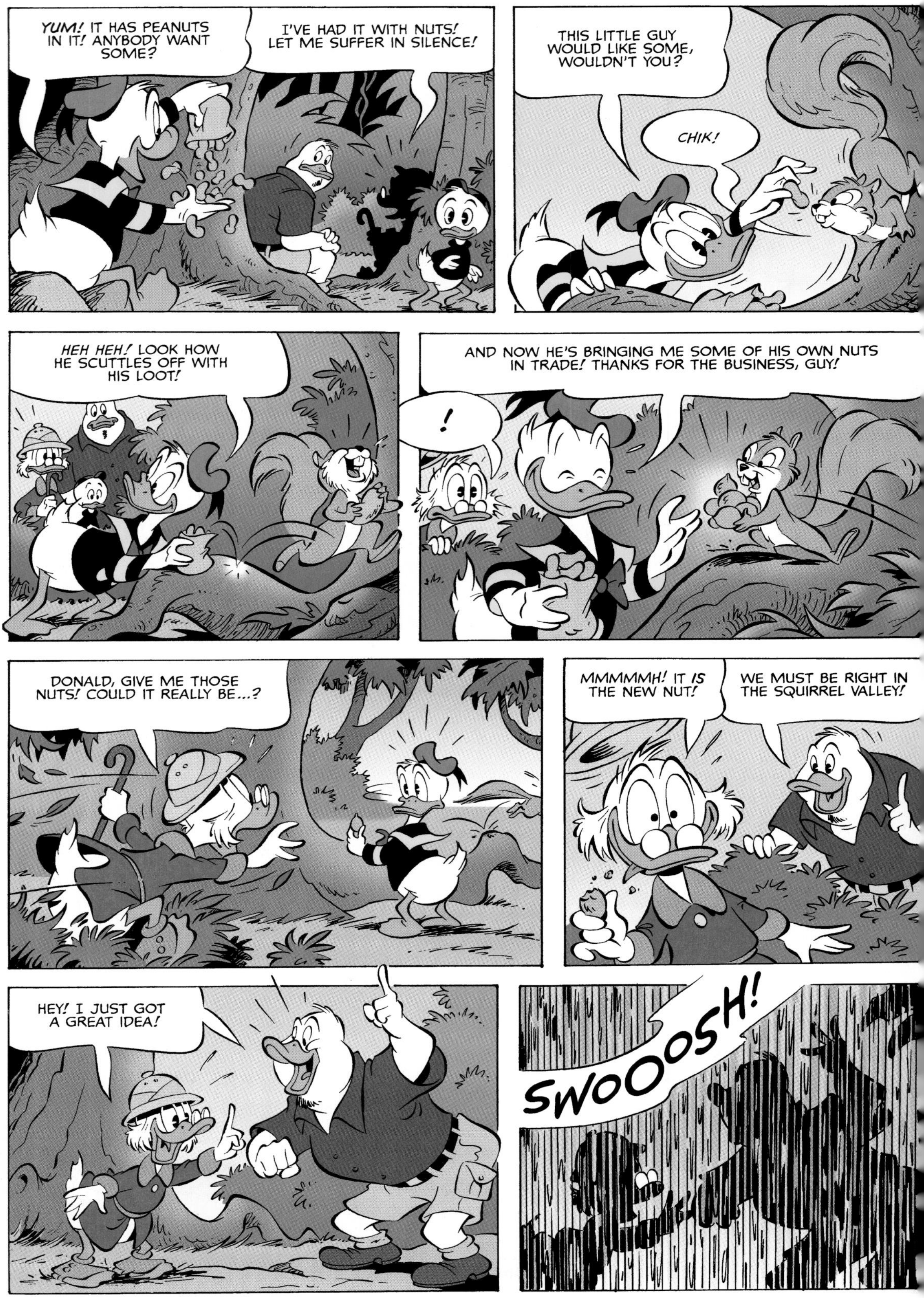
YUM! IT HAS PEANUTS IN IT! ANYBODY WANT SOME?
I'VE HAD IT WITH NUTS! LET ME SUFFER IN SILENCE!
THIS LITTLE GUY WOULD LIKE SOME, WOULDN'T YOU?
CHIK!
HEH HEH! LOOK HOW HE SCUTTLES OFF WITH HIS LOOT!
AND NOW HE'S BRINGING ME SOME OF HIS OWN NUTS IN TRADE! THANKS FOR THE BUSINESS, GUY!
!
DONALD, GIVE ME THOSE NUTS! COULD IT REALLY BE...?
MMMMMH! IT IS THE NEW NUT!
WE MUST BE RIGHT IN THE SQUIRREL VALLEY!
HEY! I JUST GOT A GREAT IDEA!
SWOOOSH!

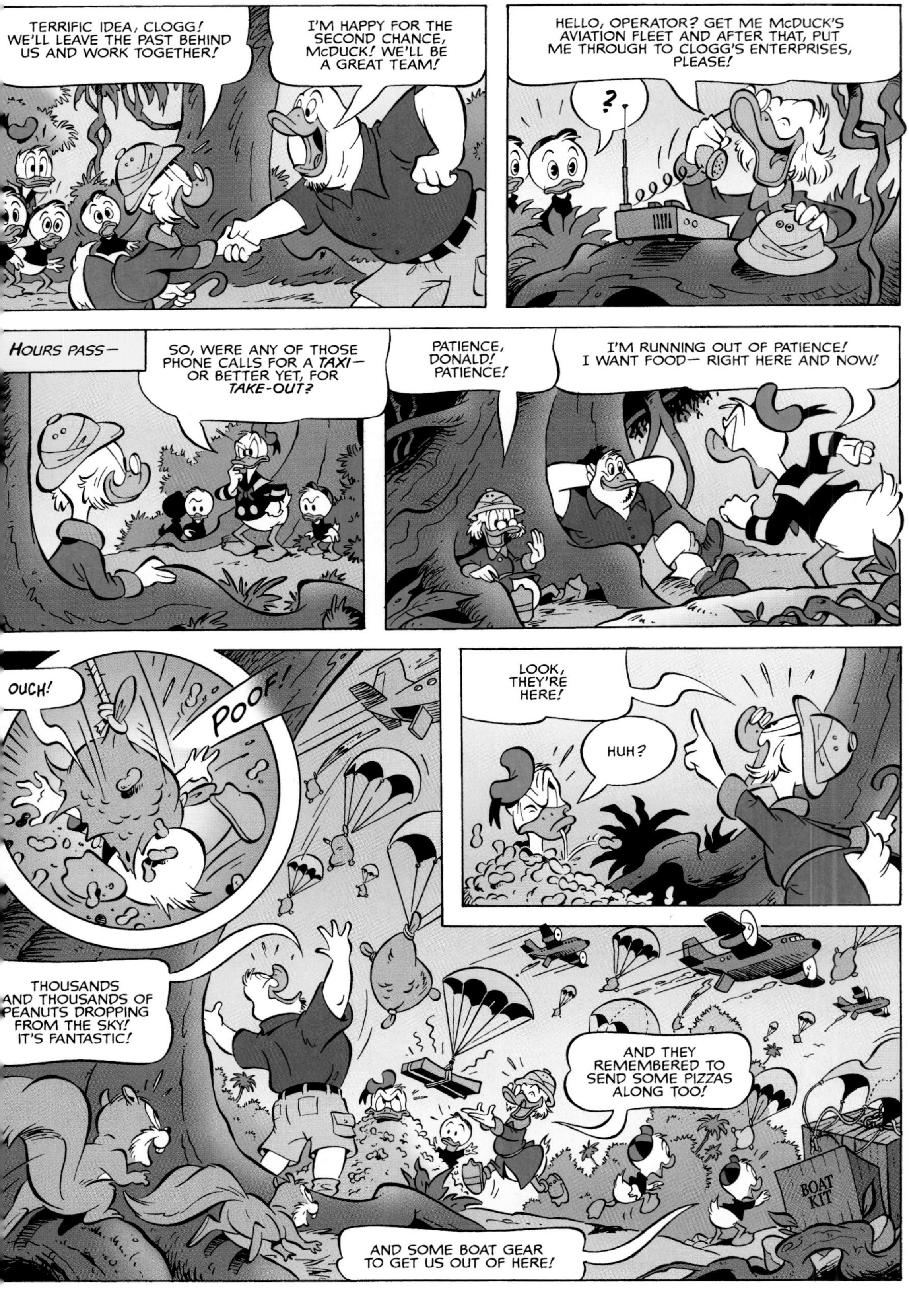

TERRIFIC IDEA, CLOGG! WE'LL LEAVE THE PAST BEHIND US AND WORK TOGETHER!
I'M HAPPY FOR THE SECOND CHANCE, McDUCK! WE'LL BE A GREAT TEAM!
HELLO, OPERATOR? GET ME McDUCK'S AVIATION FLEET AND AFTER THAT, PUT ME THROUGH TO CLOGG'S ENTERPRISES, PLEASE!
?
HOURS PASS—
SO, WERE ANY OF THOSE PHONE CALLS FOR A *TAXI*— OR BETTER YET, FOR *TAKE-OUT?*
PATIENCE, DONALD! PATIENCE!
I'M RUNNING OUT OF PATIENCE! I WANT FOOD— RIGHT HERE AND NOW!
OUCH!
POOF!
LOOK, THEY'RE HERE!
HUH?
THOUSANDS AND THOUSANDS OF PEANUTS DROPPING FROM THE SKY! IT'S FANTASTIC!
AND THEY REMEMBERED TO SEND SOME PIZZAS ALONG TOO!
AND SOME BOAT GEAR TO GET US OUT OF HERE!
BOAT KIT

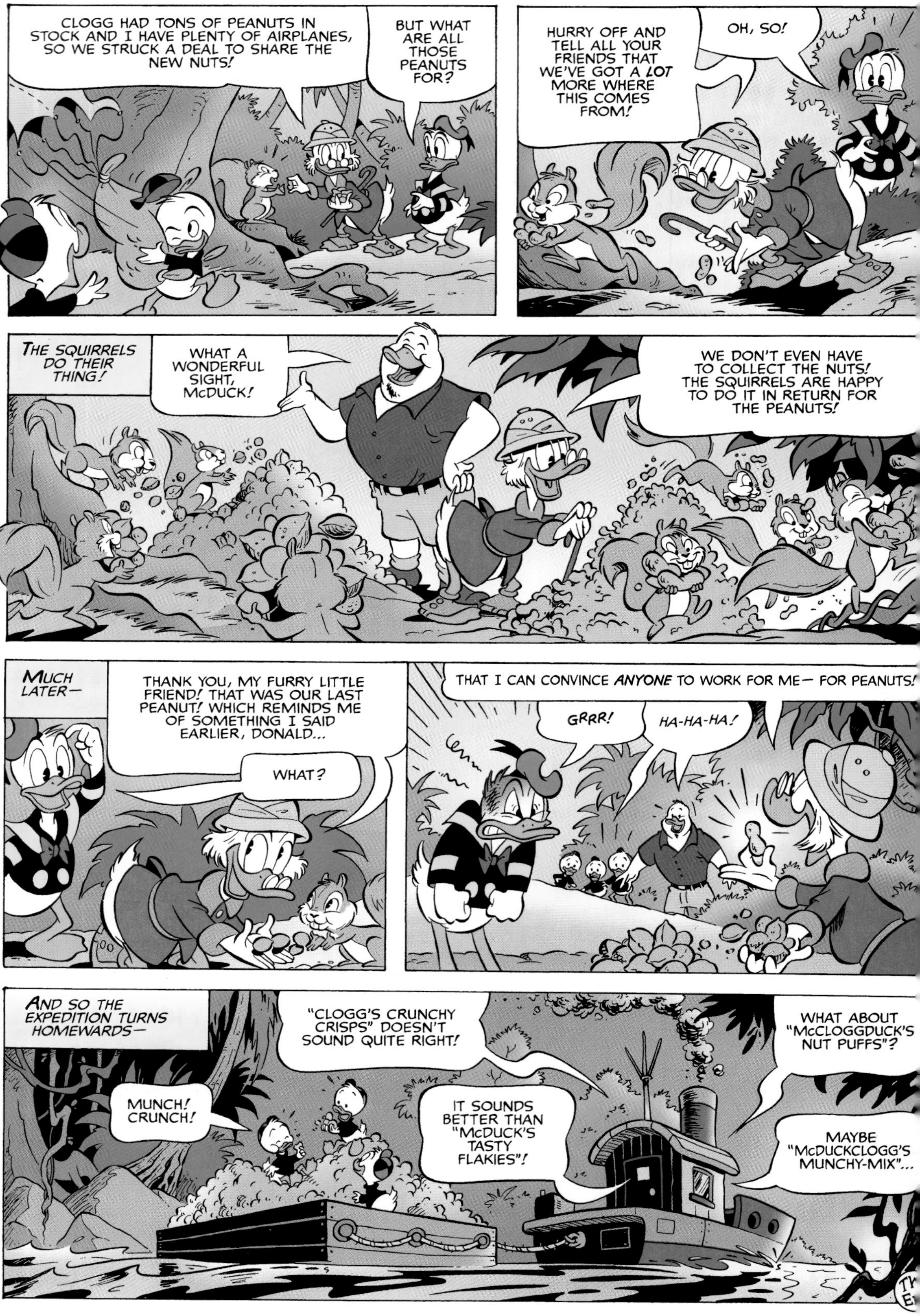
CLOGG HAD TONS OF PEANUTS IN STOCK AND I HAVE PLENTY OF AIRPLANES, SO WE STRUCK A DEAL TO SHARE THE NEW NUTS!
BUT WHAT ARE ALL THOSE PEANUTS FOR?
HURRY OFF AND TELL ALL YOUR FRIENDS THAT WE'VE GOT A LOT MORE WHERE THIS COMES FROM!
OH, SO!
THE SQUIRRELS DO THEIR THING!
WHAT A WONDERFUL SIGHT, McDUCK!
WE DON'T EVEN HAVE TO COLLECT THE NUTS! THE SQUIRRELS ARE HAPPY TO DO IT IN RETURN FOR THE PEANUTS!
MUCH LATER—
THANK YOU, MY FURRY LITTLE FRIEND! THAT WAS OUR LAST PEANUT! WHICH REMINDS ME OF SOMETHING I SAID EARLIER, DONALD...
WHAT?
THAT I CAN CONVINCE ANYONE TO WORK FOR ME— FOR PEANUTS!
GRRR!
HA-HA-HA!
AND SO THE EXPEDITION TURNS HOMEWARDS—
"CLOGG'S CRUNCHY CRISPS" DOESN'T SOUND QUITE RIGHT!
WHAT ABOUT "McCLOGGDUCK'S NUT PUFFS"?
MUNCH! CRUNCH!
IT SOUNDS BETTER THAN "McDUCK'S TASTY FLAKIES"!
MAYBE "McDUCKCLOGG'S MUNCHY-MIX"...

# Walt Disney's Huey, Dewey & Louie in THE SECRET FISHING HOLE

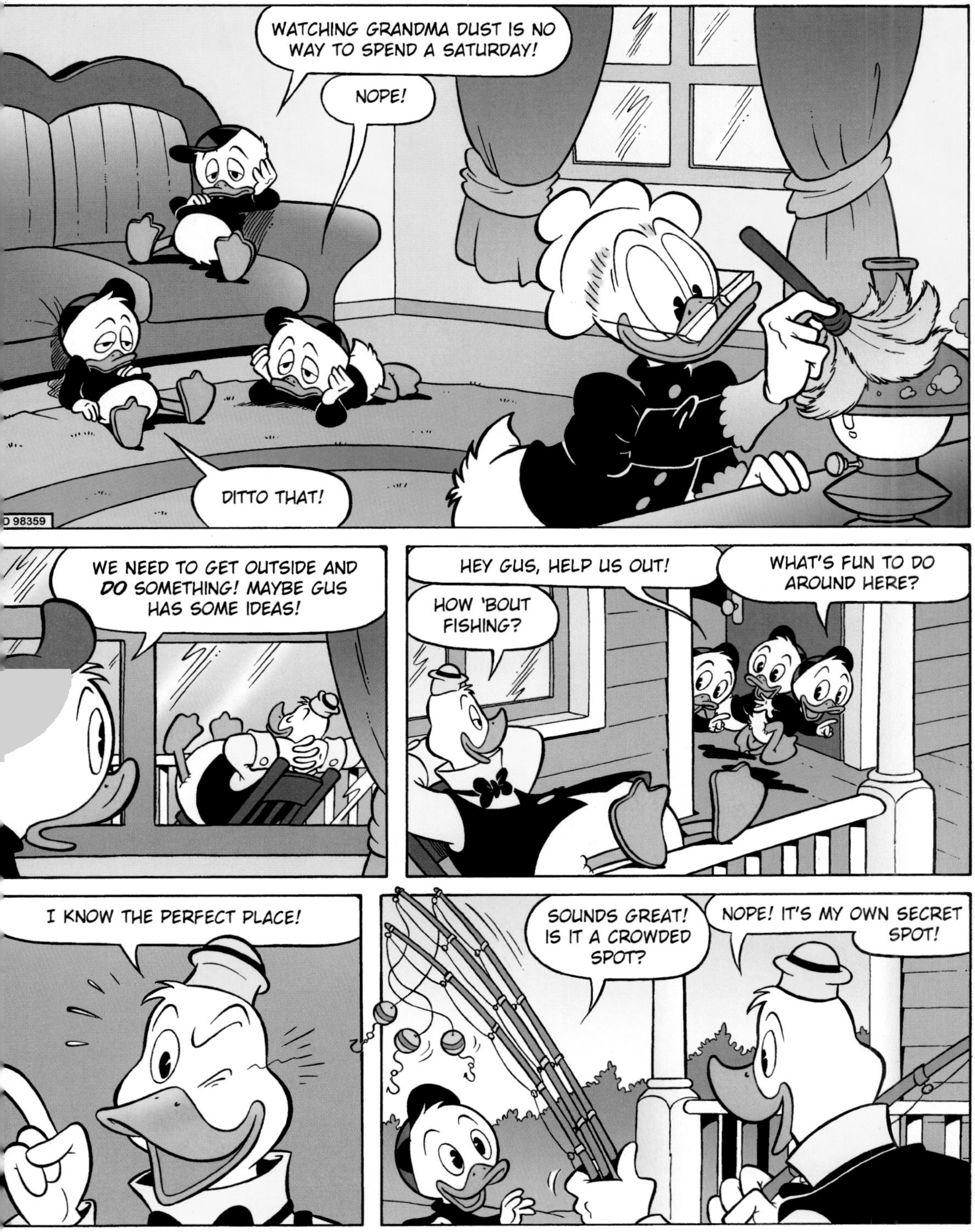

WATCHING GRANDMA DUST IS NO WAY TO SPEND A SATURDAY!
NOPE!
DITTO THAT!
D 98359
WE NEED TO GET OUTSIDE AND *DO* SOMETHING! MAYBE GUS HAS SOME IDEAS!
HEY GUS, HELP US OUT!
WHAT'S FUN TO DO AROUND HERE?
HOW 'BOUT FISHING?
I KNOW THE PERFECT PLACE!
SOUNDS GREAT! IS IT A CROWDED SPOT?
NOPE! IT'S MY OWN SECRET SPOT!

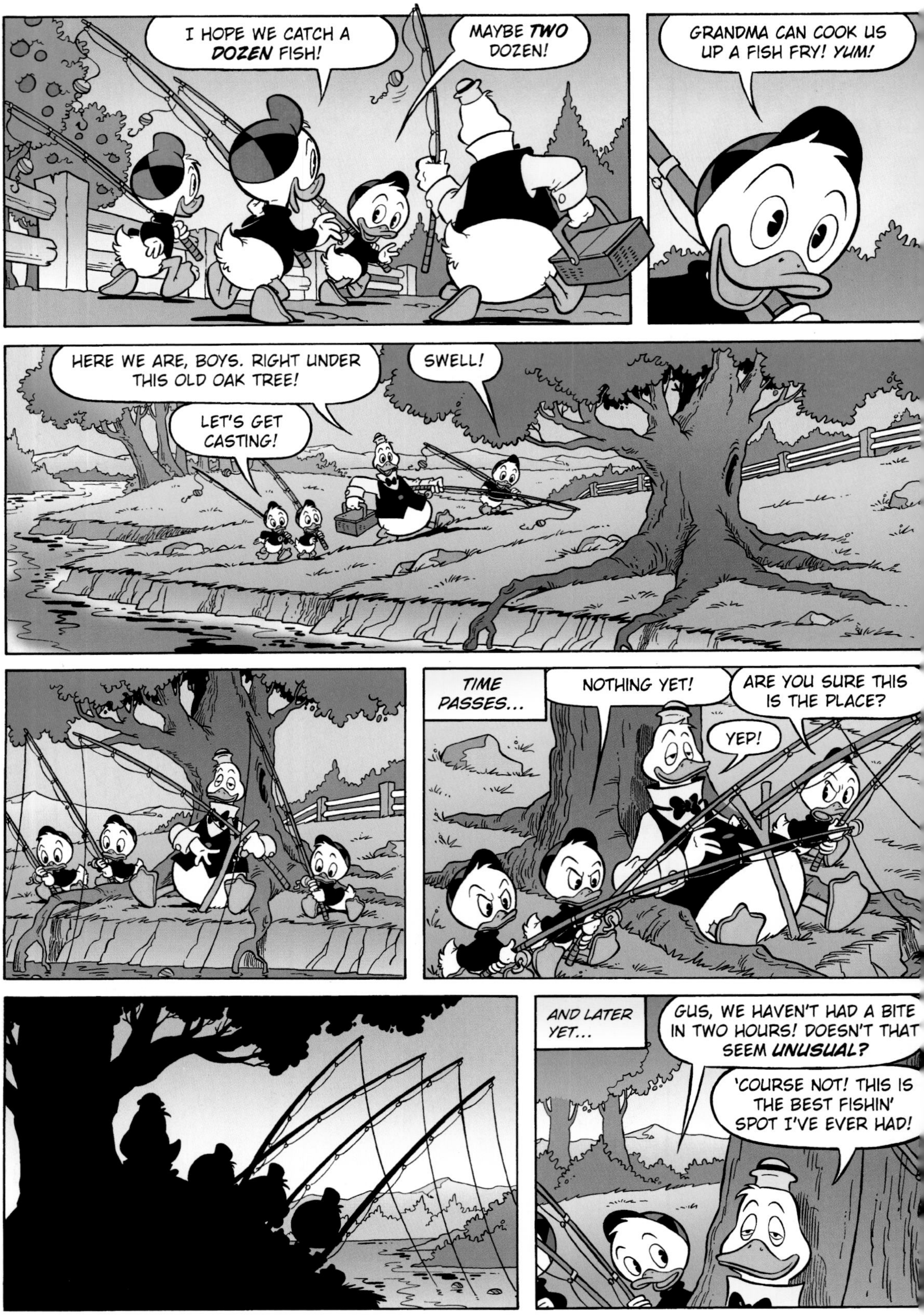
I HOPE WE CATCH A DOZEN FISH!
MAYBE TWO DOZEN!
GRANDMA CAN COOK US UP A FISH FRY! YUM!
HERE WE ARE, BOYS. RIGHT UNDER THIS OLD OAK TREE!
SWELL!
LET'S GET CASTING!
TIME PASSES...
NOTHING YET!
ARE YOU SURE THIS IS THE PLACE?
YEP!
AND LATER YET...
GUS, WE HAVEN'T HAD A BITE IN TWO HOURS! DOESN'T THAT SEEM UNUSUAL?
'COURSE NOT! THIS IS THE BEST FISHIN' SPOT I'VE EVER HAD!

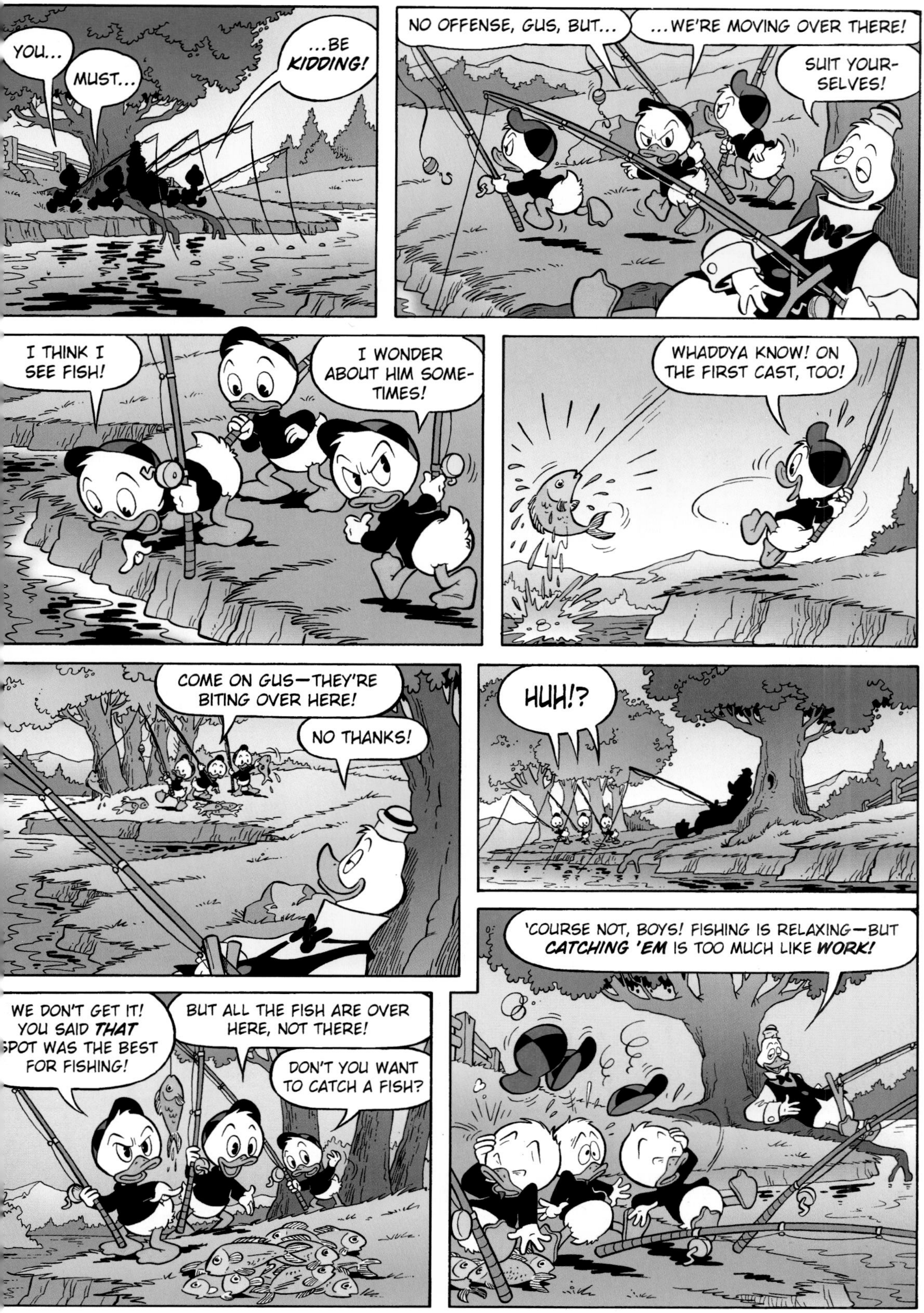

YOU...
MUST...
...BE KIDDING!
NO OFFENSE, GUS, BUT...
...WE'RE MOVING OVER THERE!
SUIT YOURSELVES!
I THINK I SEE FISH!
I WONDER ABOUT HIM SOMETIMES!
WHADDYA KNOW! ON THE FIRST CAST, TOO!
COME ON GUS—THEY'RE BITING OVER HERE!
NO THANKS!
HUH!?
WE DON'T GET IT! YOU SAID THAT SPOT WAS THE BEST FOR FISHING!
BUT ALL THE FISH ARE OVER HERE, NOT THERE!
DON'T YOU WANT TO CATCH A FISH?
'COURSE NOT, BOYS! FISHING IS RELAXING—BUT CATCHING 'EM IS TOO MUCH LIKE WORK!

# FREE COMIC BOOK · DAY ·

## SATURDAY, JULY 3
### www.freecomicbookday.com

## ASK ABOUT YOUR FREE COMIC BOOK

**At Participating Retailers Only**

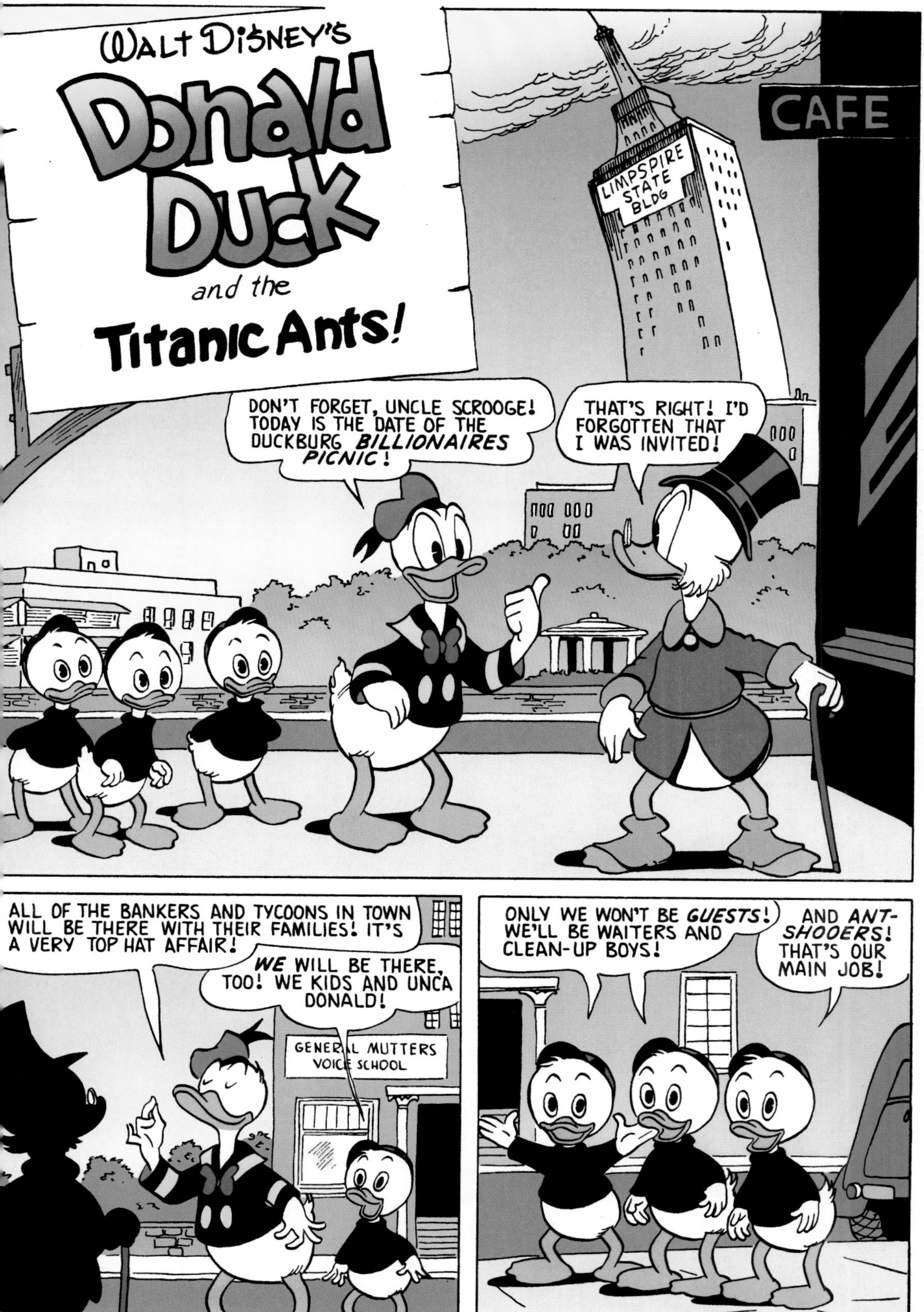
WALT DISNEY'S
Donald Duck
and the
Titanic Ants!
CAFE
LIMPSPIRE STATE BLDG
DON'T FORGET, UNCLE SCROOGE! TODAY IS THE DATE OF THE DUCKBURG BILLIONAIRES PICNIC!
THAT'S RIGHT! I'D FORGOTTEN THAT I WAS INVITED!
ALL OF THE BANKERS AND TYCOONS IN TOWN WILL BE THERE WITH THEIR FAMILIES! IT'S A VERY TOP HAT AFFAIR!
WE WILL BE THERE, TOO! WE KIDS AND UNCA DONALD!
GENERAL MUTTERS VOICE SCHOOL
ONLY WE WON'T BE GUESTS! WE'LL BE WAITERS AND CLEAN-UP BOYS!
AND ANT-SHOOERS! THAT'S OUR MAIN JOB!

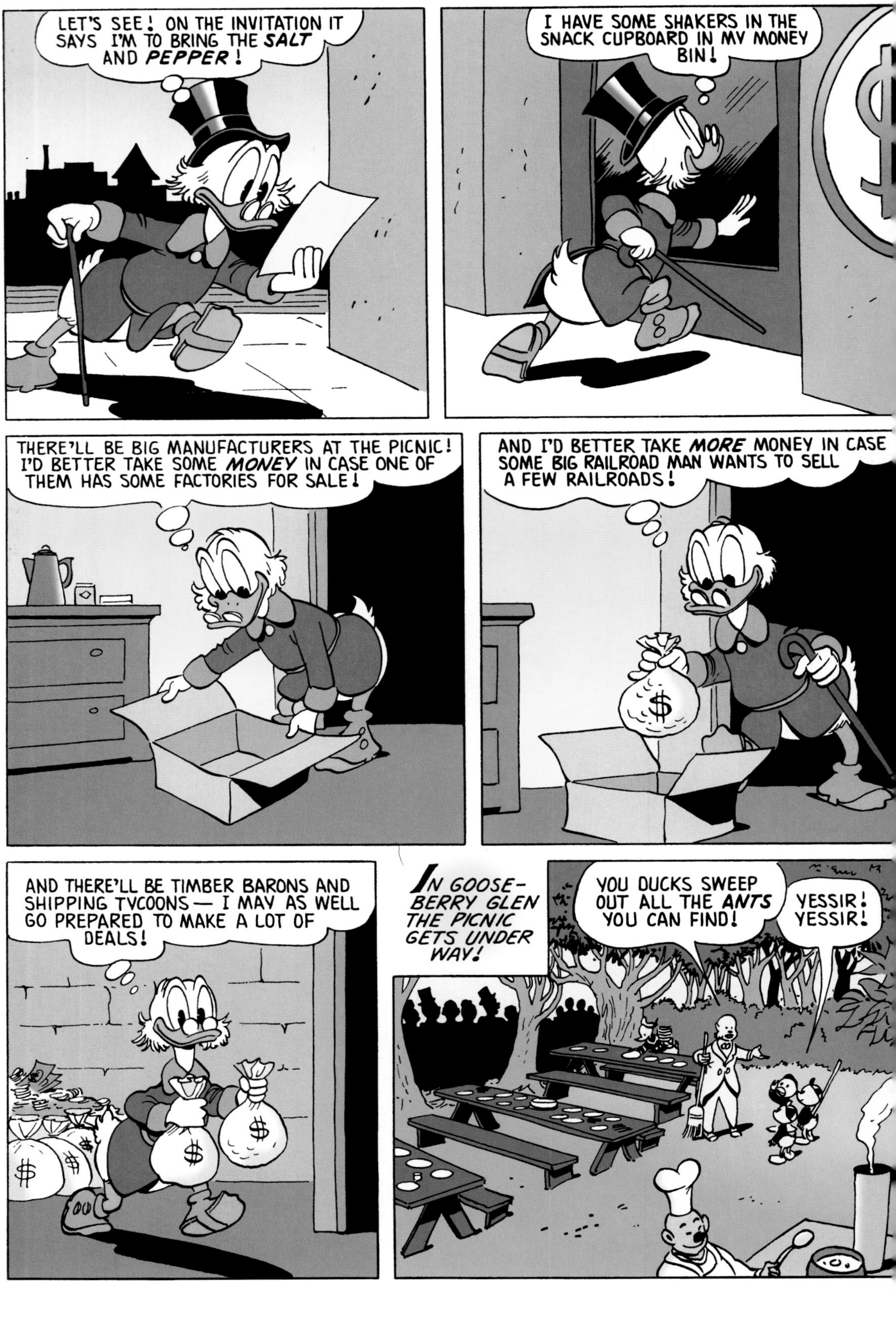
LET'S SEE! ON THE INVITATION IT SAYS I'M TO BRING THE SALT AND PEPPER!
I HAVE SOME SHAKERS IN THE SNACK CUPBOARD IN MY MONEY BIN!
THERE'LL BE BIG MANUFACTURERS AT THE PICNIC! I'D BETTER TAKE SOME MONEY IN CASE ONE OF THEM HAS SOME FACTORIES FOR SALE!
AND I'D BETTER TAKE MORE MONEY IN CASE SOME BIG RAILROAD MAN WANTS TO SELL A FEW RAILROADS!
AND THERE'LL BE TIMBER BARONS AND SHIPPING TYCOONS — I MAY AS WELL GO PREPARED TO MAKE A LOT OF DEALS!
IN GOOSEBERRY GLEN THE PICNIC GETS UNDER WAY!
YOU DUCKS SWEEP OUT ALL THE ANTS YOU CAN FIND!
YESSIR! YESSIR!

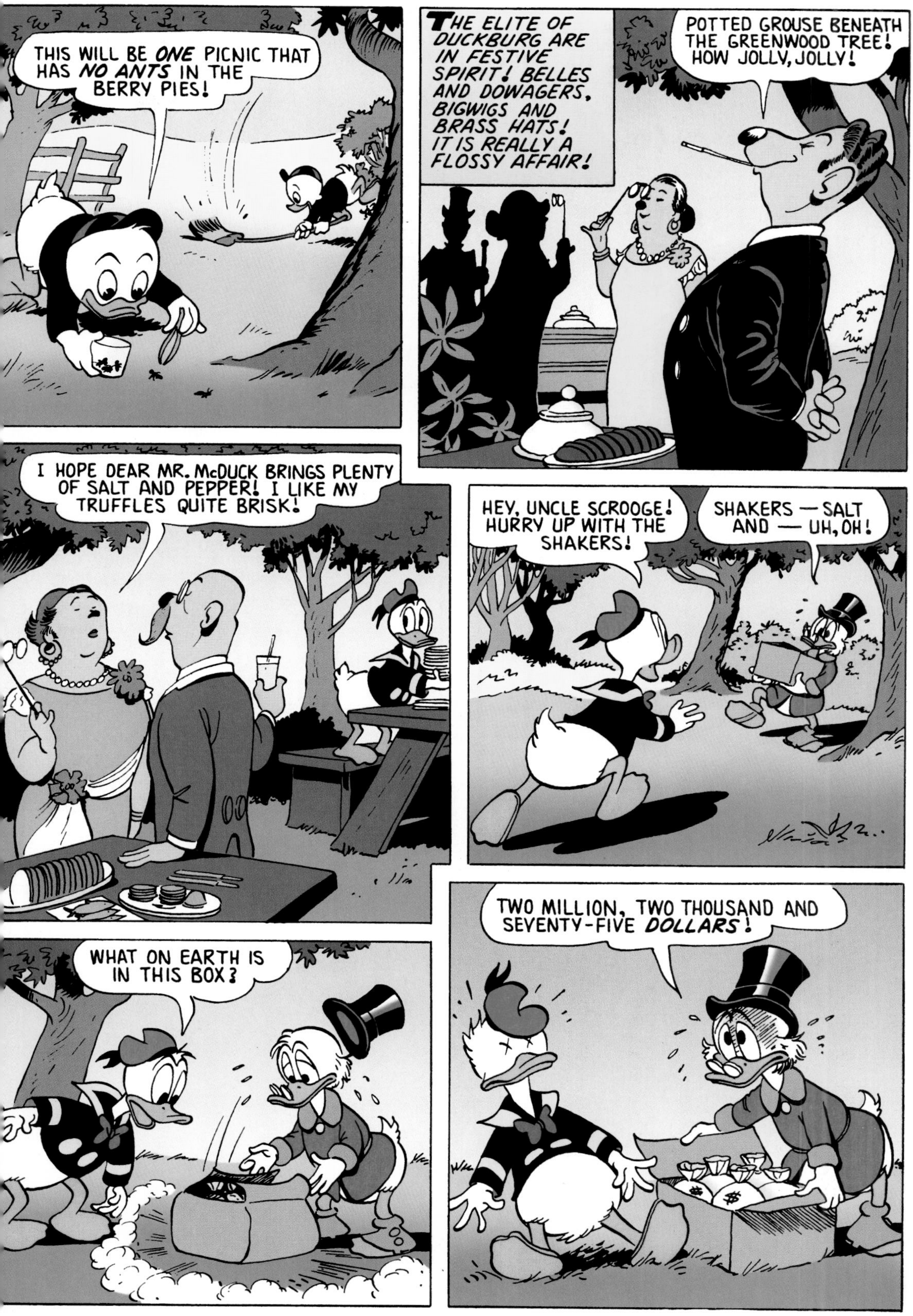
THIS WILL BE ONE PICNIC THAT HAS NO ANTS IN THE BERRY PIES!
THE ELITE OF DUCKBURG ARE IN FESTIVE SPIRIT! BELLES AND DOWAGERS, BIGWIGS AND BRASS HATS! IT IS REALLY A FLOSSY AFFAIR!
POTTED GROUSE BENEATH THE GREENWOOD TREE! HOW JOLLY, JOLLY!
I HOPE DEAR MR. McDUCK BRINGS PLENTY OF SALT AND PEPPER! I LIKE MY TRUFFLES QUITE BRISK!
HEY, UNCLE SCROOGE! HURRY UP WITH THE SHAKERS!
SHAKERS — SALT AND — UH, OH!
WHAT ON EARTH IS IN THIS BOX?
TWO MILLION, TWO THOUSAND AND SEVENTY-FIVE DOLLARS!

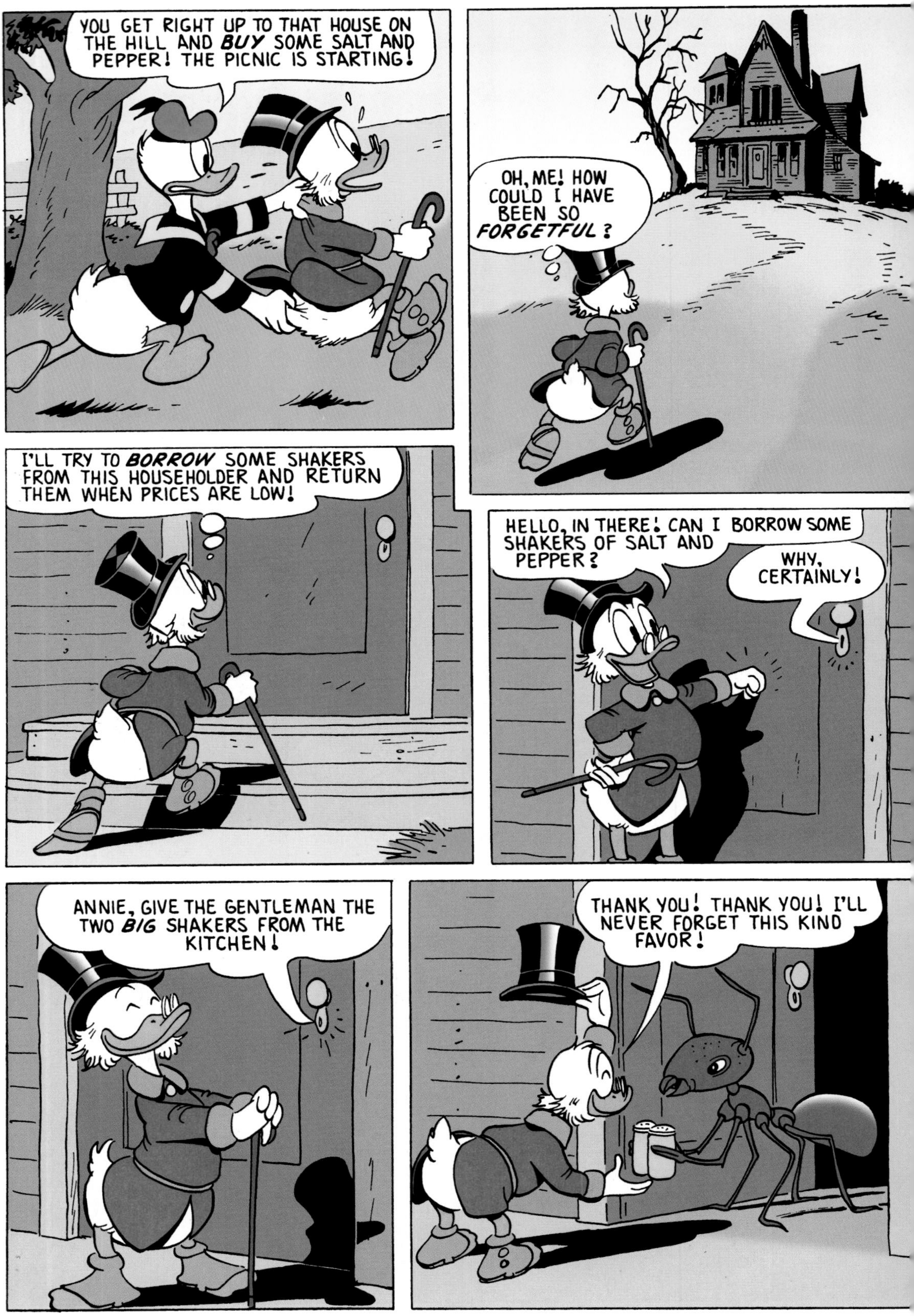
YOU GET RIGHT UP TO THAT HOUSE ON THE HILL AND *BUY* SOME SALT AND PEPPER! THE PICNIC IS STARTING!
OH, ME! HOW COULD I HAVE BEEN SO *FORGETFUL*?
I'LL TRY TO *BORROW* SOME SHAKERS FROM THIS HOUSEHOLDER AND RETURN THEM WHEN PRICES ARE LOW!
HELLO, IN THERE! CAN I BORROW SOME SHAKERS OF SALT AND PEPPER?
WHY, CERTAINLY!
ANNIE, GIVE THE GENTLEMAN THE TWO *BIG* SHAKERS FROM THE KITCHEN!
THANK YOU! THANK YOU! I'LL NEVER FORGET THIS KIND FAVOR!

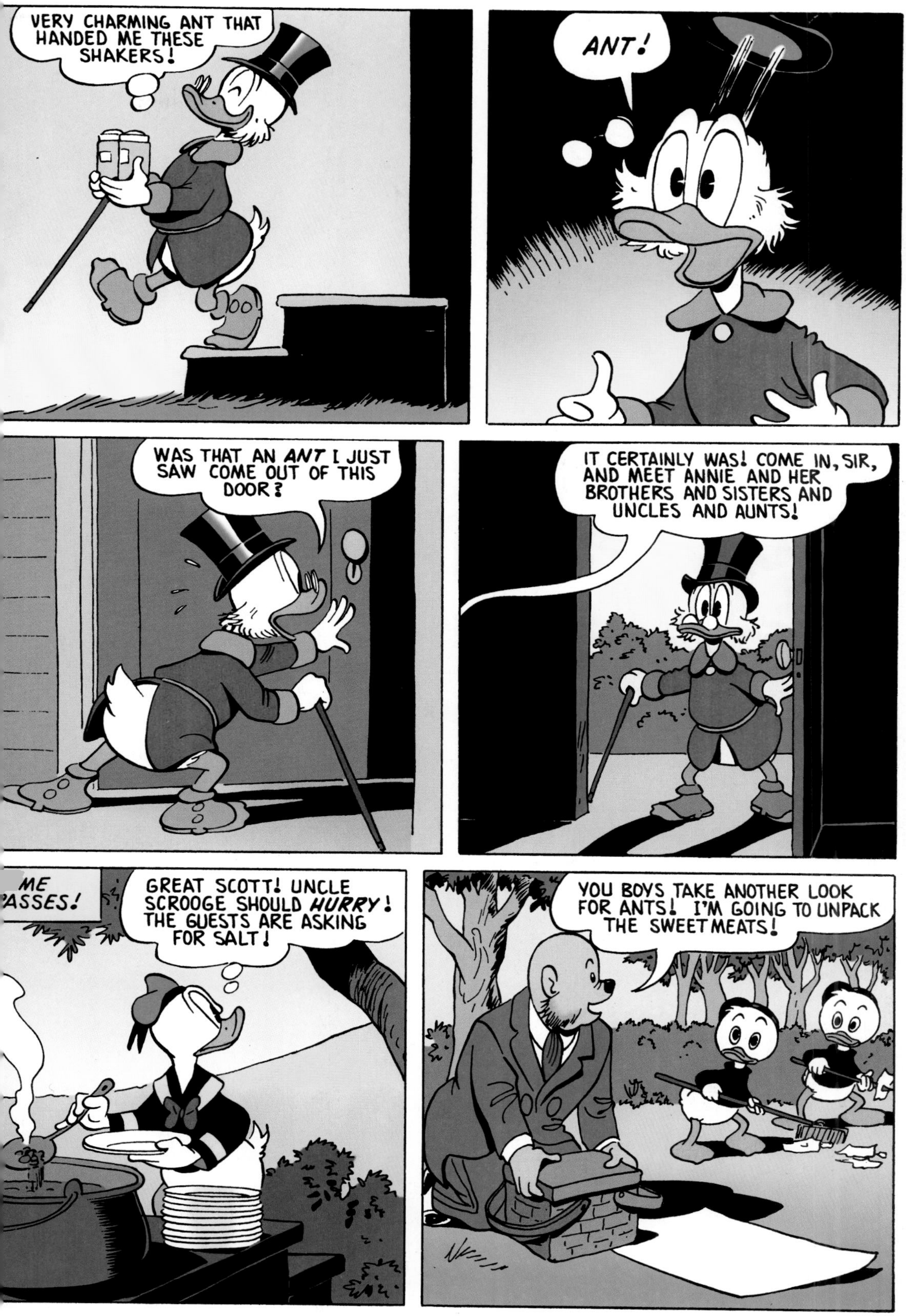

VERY CHARMING ANT THAT HANDED ME THESE SHAKERS!
ANT!
WAS THAT AN *ANT* I JUST SAW COME OUT OF THIS DOOR?
IT CERTAINLY WAS! COME IN, SIR, AND MEET ANNIE AND HER BROTHERS AND SISTERS AND UNCLES AND AUNTS!
ME
ASSES!
GREAT SCOTT! UNCLE SCROOGE SHOULD *HURRY*! THE GUESTS ARE ASKING FOR SALT!
YOU BOYS TAKE ANOTHER LOOK FOR ANTS! I'M GOING TO UNPACK THE SWEETMEATS!

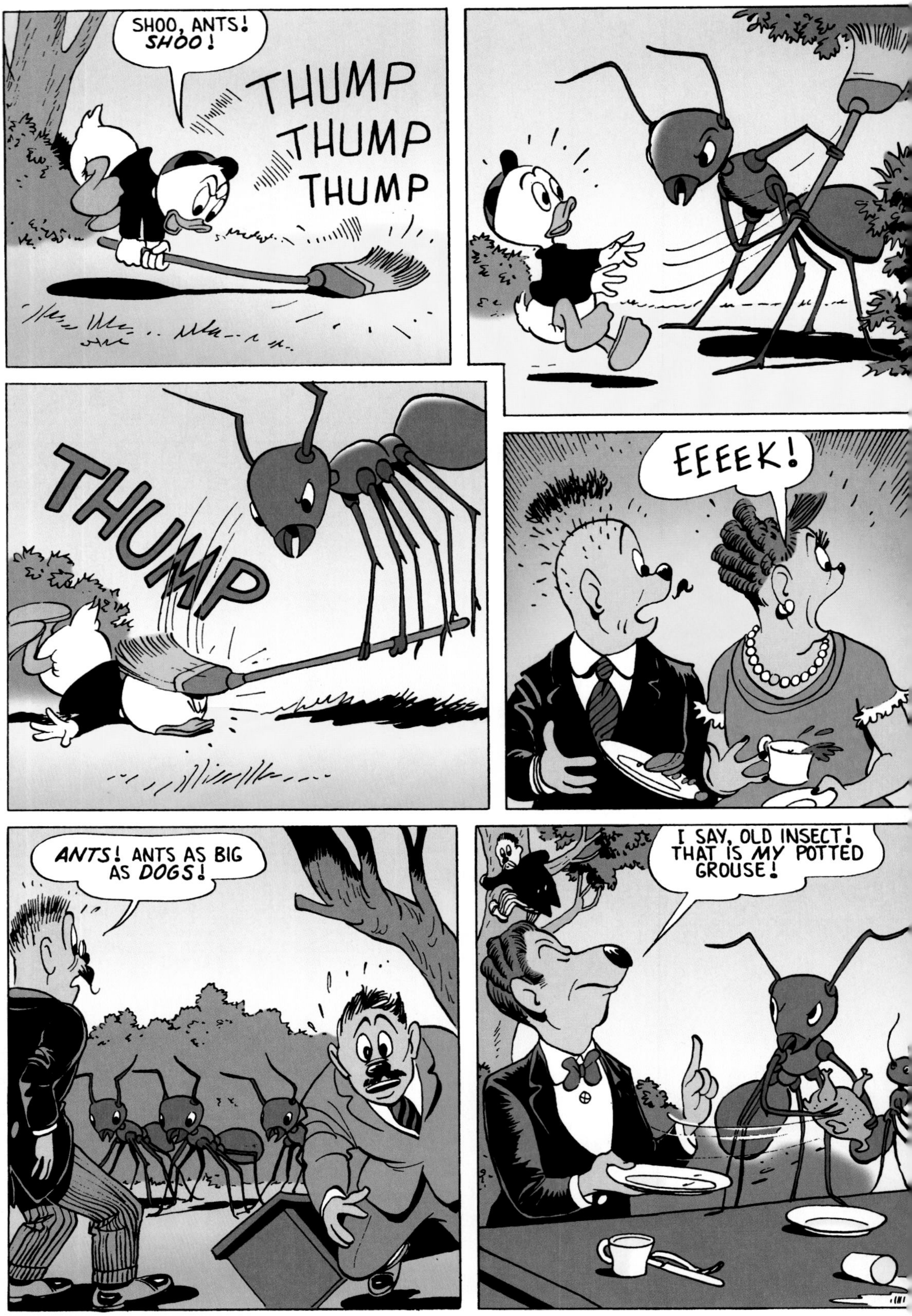
SHOO, ANTS! SHOO!
THUMP THUMP THUMP
THUMP
EEEEK!
ANTS! ANTS AS BIG AS DOGS!
I SAY, OLD INSECT! THAT IS MY POTTED GROUSE!

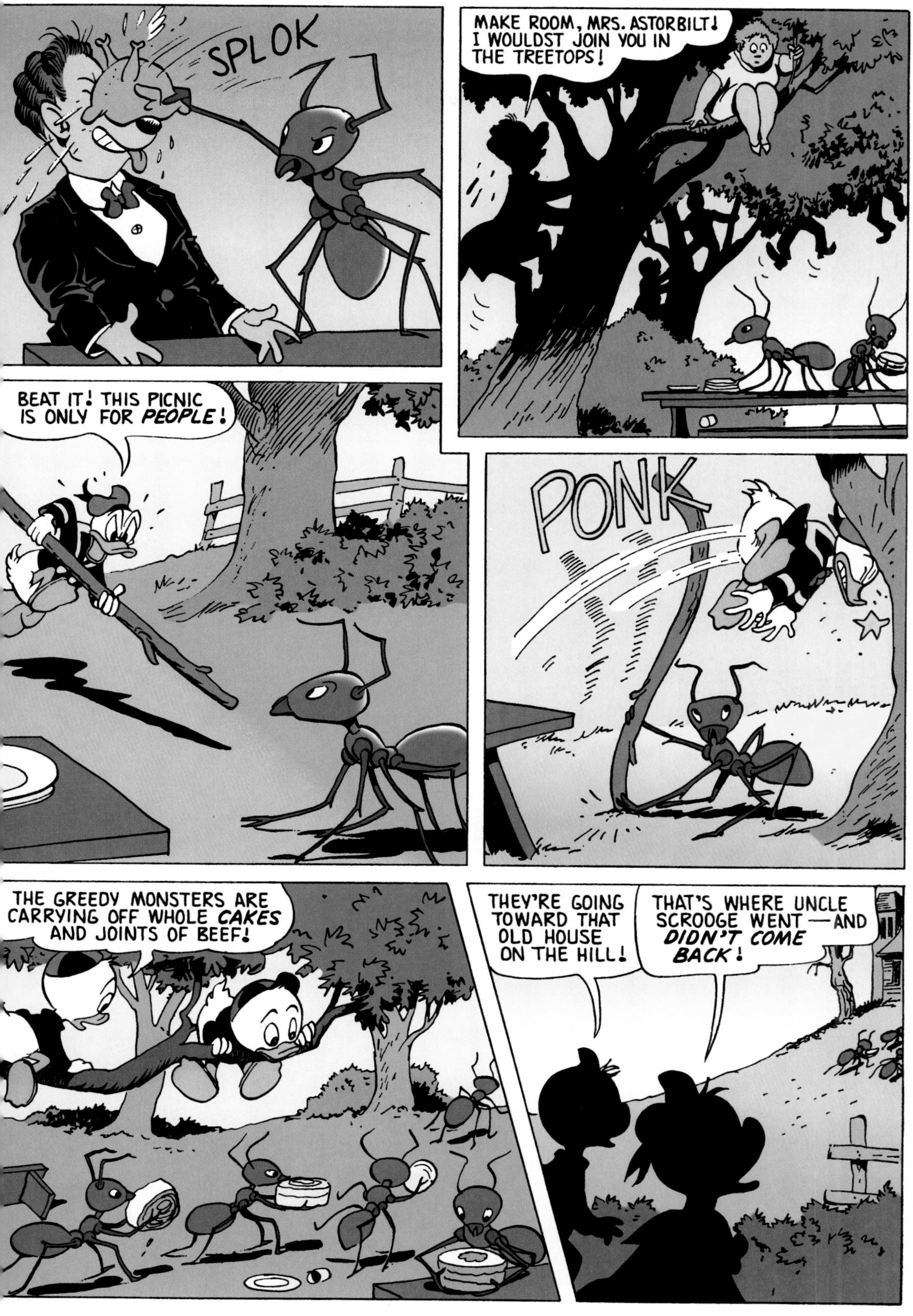
SPLOK
MAKE ROOM, MRS. ASTORBILT! I WOULDST JOIN YOU IN THE TREETOPS!
BEAT IT! THIS PICNIC IS ONLY FOR *PEOPLE*!
PONK
THE GREEDY MONSTERS ARE CARRYING OFF WHOLE *CAKES* AND JOINTS OF BEEF!
THEY'RE GOING TOWARD THAT OLD HOUSE ON THE HILL!
THAT'S WHERE UNCLE SCROOGE WENT — AND *DIDN'T COME BACK*!

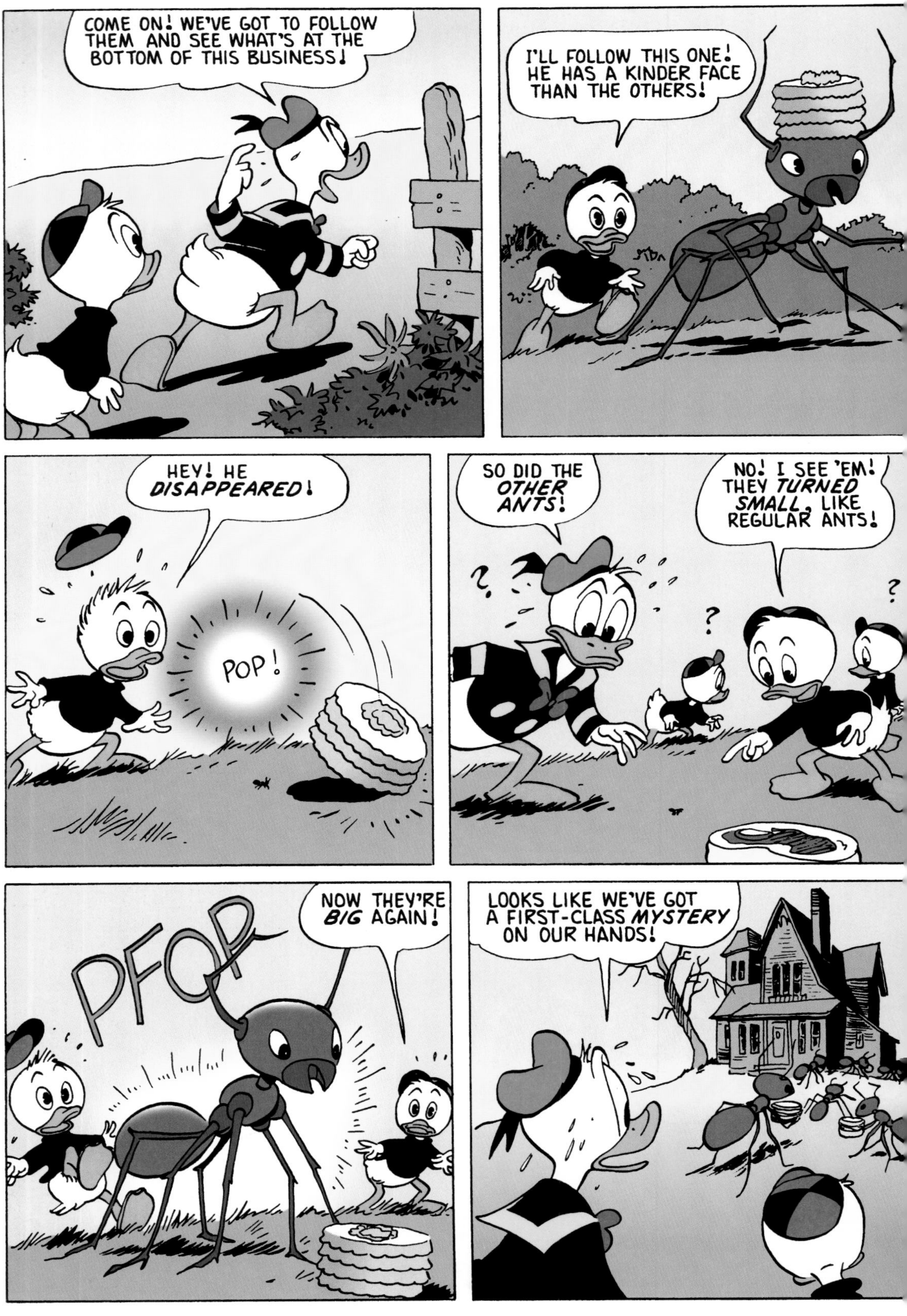
COME ON! WE'VE GOT TO FOLLOW THEM AND SEE WHAT'S AT THE BOTTOM OF THIS BUSINESS!
I'LL FOLLOW THIS ONE! HE HAS A KINDER FACE THAN THE OTHERS!
HEY! HE DISAPPEARED!
POP!
SO DID THE OTHER ANTS!
NO! I SEE 'EM! THEY TURNED SMALL, LIKE REGULAR ANTS!
PFOP
NOW THEY'RE BIG AGAIN!
LOOKS LIKE WE'VE GOT A FIRST-CLASS MYSTERY ON OUR HANDS!

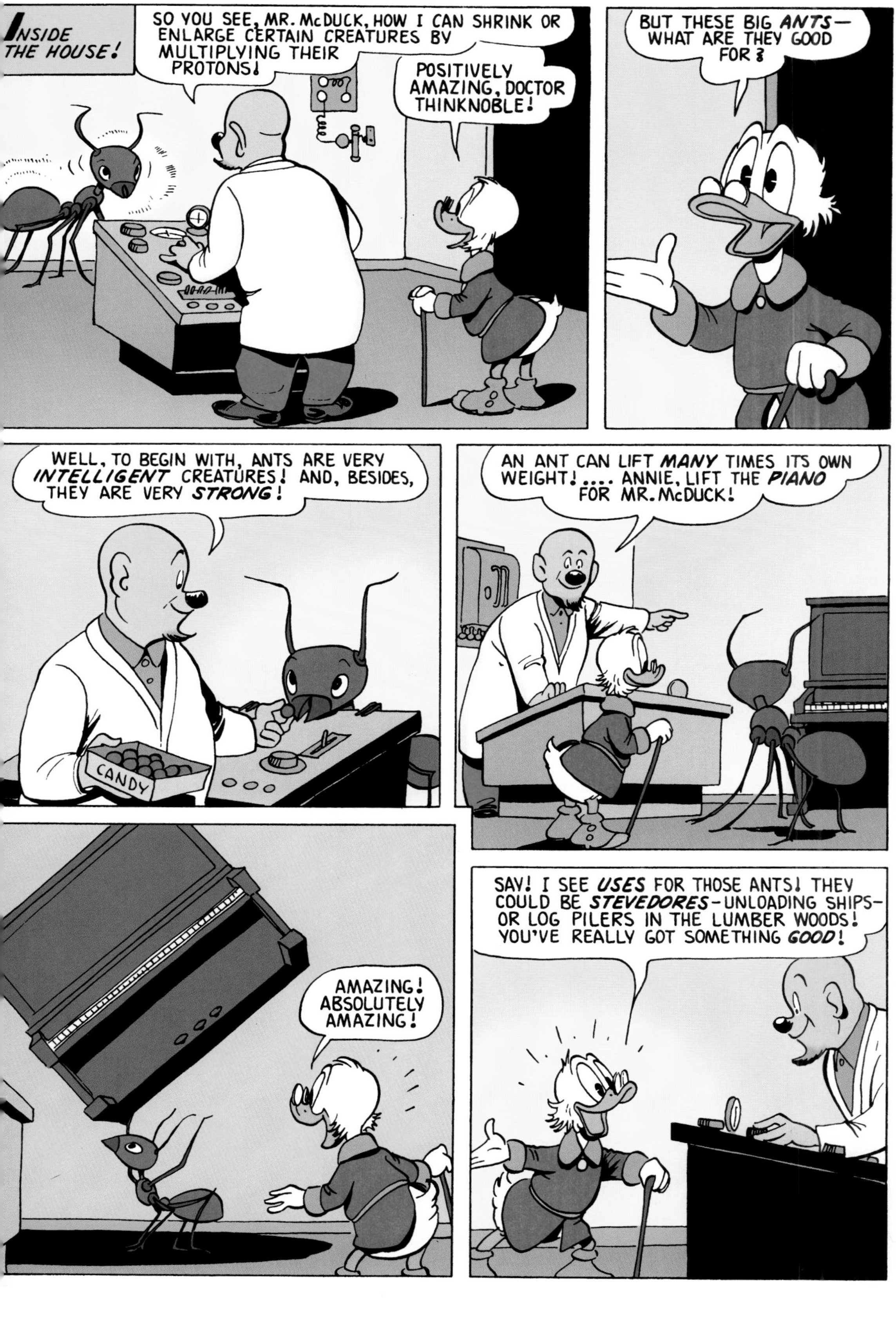
INSIDE THE HOUSE!
SO YOU SEE, MR. McDUCK, HOW I CAN SHRINK OR ENLARGE CERTAIN CREATURES BY MULTIPLYING THEIR PROTONS!
POSITIVELY AMAZING, DOCTOR THINKNOBLE!
BUT THESE BIG *ANTS*— WHAT ARE THEY GOOD FOR?
WELL, TO BEGIN WITH, ANTS ARE VERY *INTELLIGENT* CREATURES! AND, BESIDES, THEY ARE VERY *STRONG*!
CANDY
AN ANT CAN LIFT *MANY* TIMES ITS OWN WEIGHT! .... ANNIE, LIFT THE *PIANO* FOR MR. McDUCK!
AMAZING! ABSOLUTELY AMAZING!
SAY! I SEE *USES* FOR THOSE ANTS! THEY COULD BE *STEVEDORES*—UNLOADING SHIPS—OR LOG PILERS IN THE LUMBER WOODS! YOU'VE REALLY GOT SOMETHING *GOOD*!

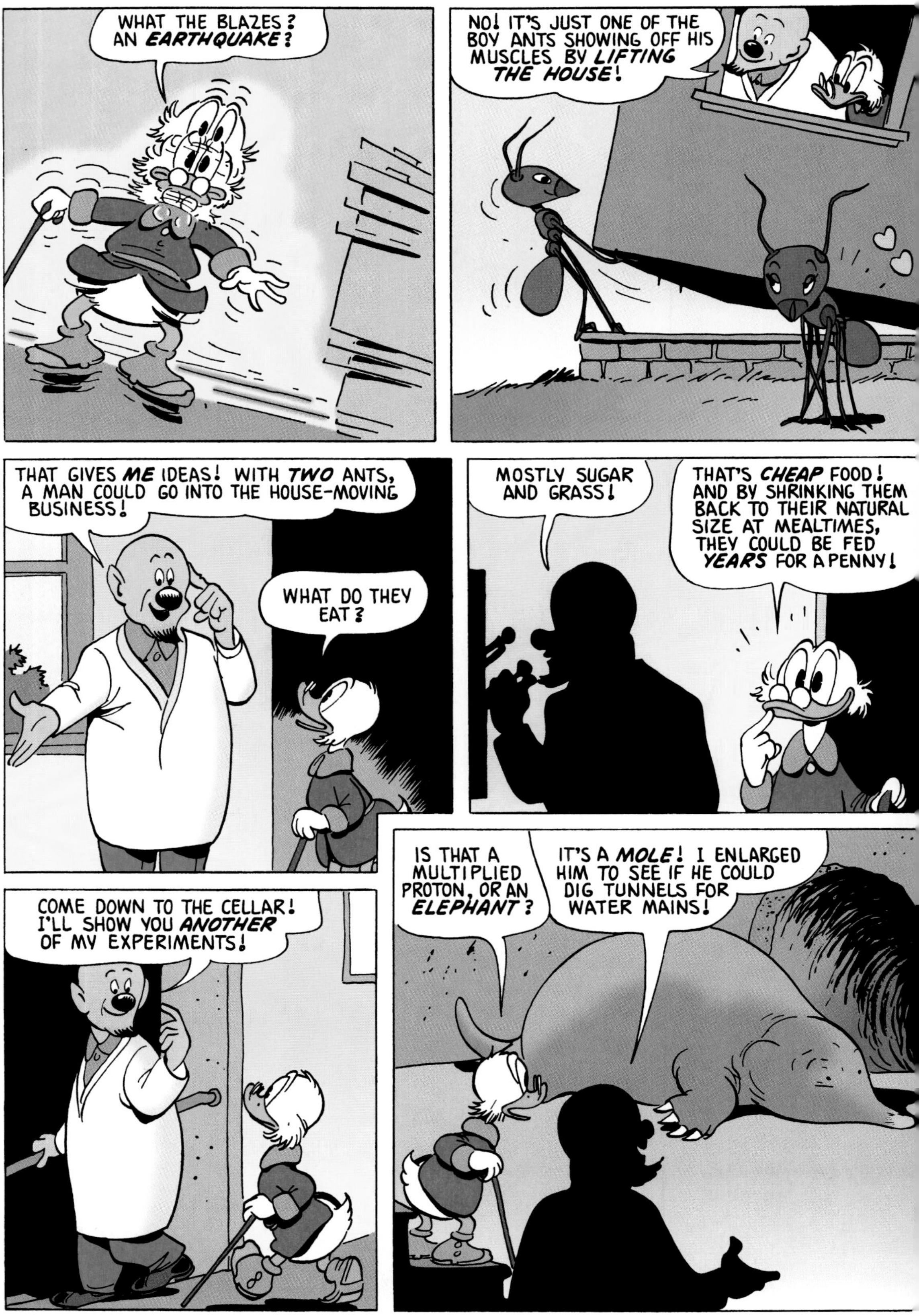
WHAT THE BLAZES? AN EARTHQUAKE?
NO! IT'S JUST ONE OF THE BOY ANTS SHOWING OFF HIS MUSCLES BY LIFTING THE HOUSE!
THAT GIVES ME IDEAS! WITH TWO ANTS, A MAN COULD GO INTO THE HOUSE-MOVING BUSINESS!
WHAT DO THEY EAT?
MOSTLY SUGAR AND GRASS!
THAT'S CHEAP FOOD! AND BY SHRINKING THEM BACK TO THEIR NATURAL SIZE AT MEALTIMES, THEY COULD BE FED YEARS FOR A PENNY!
COME DOWN TO THE CELLAR! I'LL SHOW YOU ANOTHER OF MY EXPERIMENTS!
IS THAT A MULTIPLIED PROTON, OR AN ELEPHANT?
IT'S A MOLE! I ENLARGED HIM TO SEE IF HE COULD DIG TUNNELS FOR WATER MAINS!

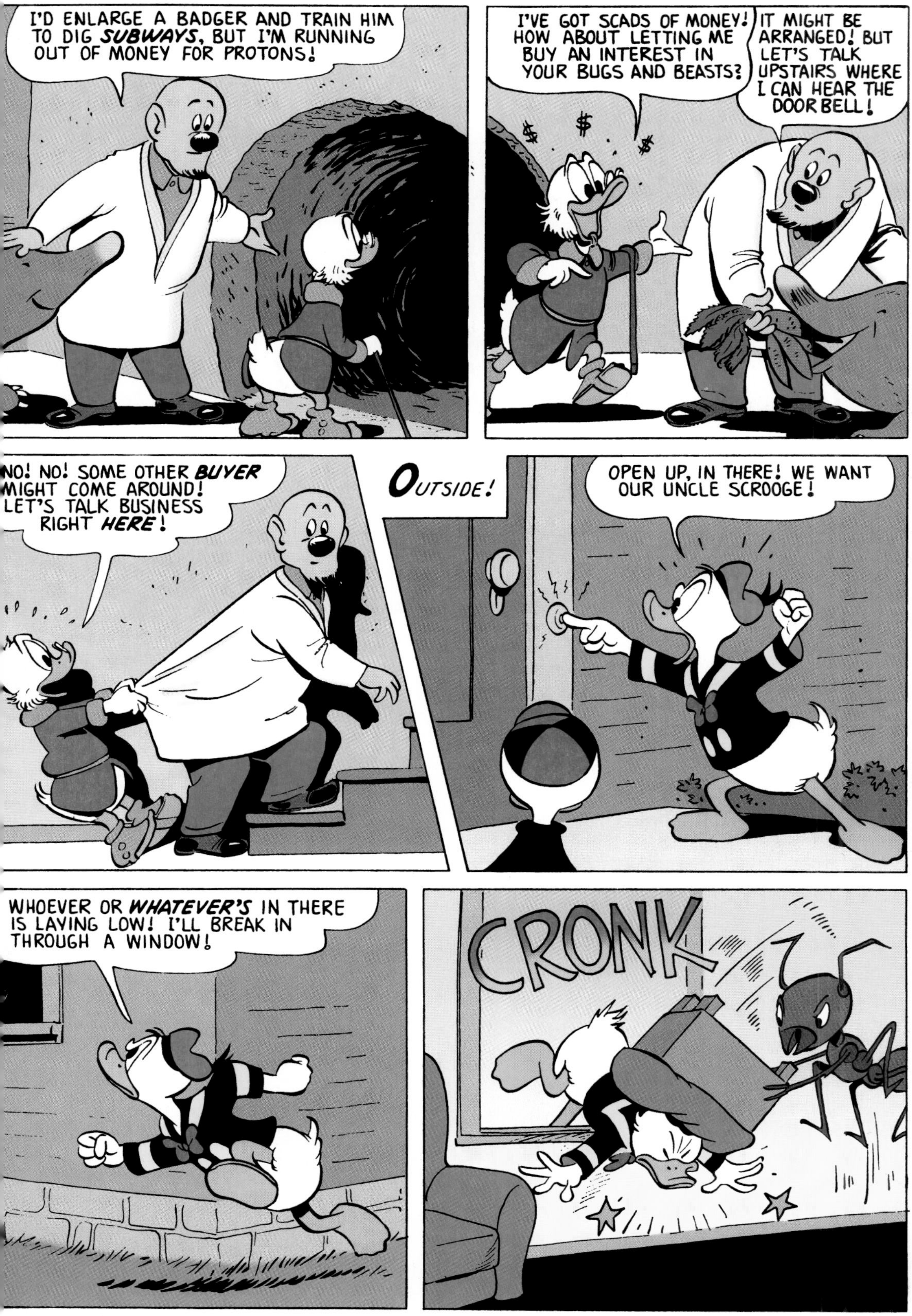
I'D ENLARGE A BADGER AND TRAIN HIM TO DIG *SUBWAYS*, BUT I'M RUNNING OUT OF MONEY FOR PROTONS!
I'VE GOT SCADS OF MONEY! HOW ABOUT LETTING ME BUY AN INTEREST IN YOUR BUGS AND BEASTS?
IT MIGHT BE ARRANGED! BUT LET'S TALK UPSTAIRS WHERE I CAN HEAR THE DOORBELL!
NO! NO! SOME OTHER *BUYER* MIGHT COME AROUND! LET'S TALK BUSINESS RIGHT *HERE*!
OUTSIDE!
OPEN UP, IN THERE! WE WANT OUR UNCLE SCROOGE!
WHOEVER OR *WHATEVER'S* IN THERE IS LAYING LOW! I'LL BREAK IN THROUGH A WINDOW!
CRONK

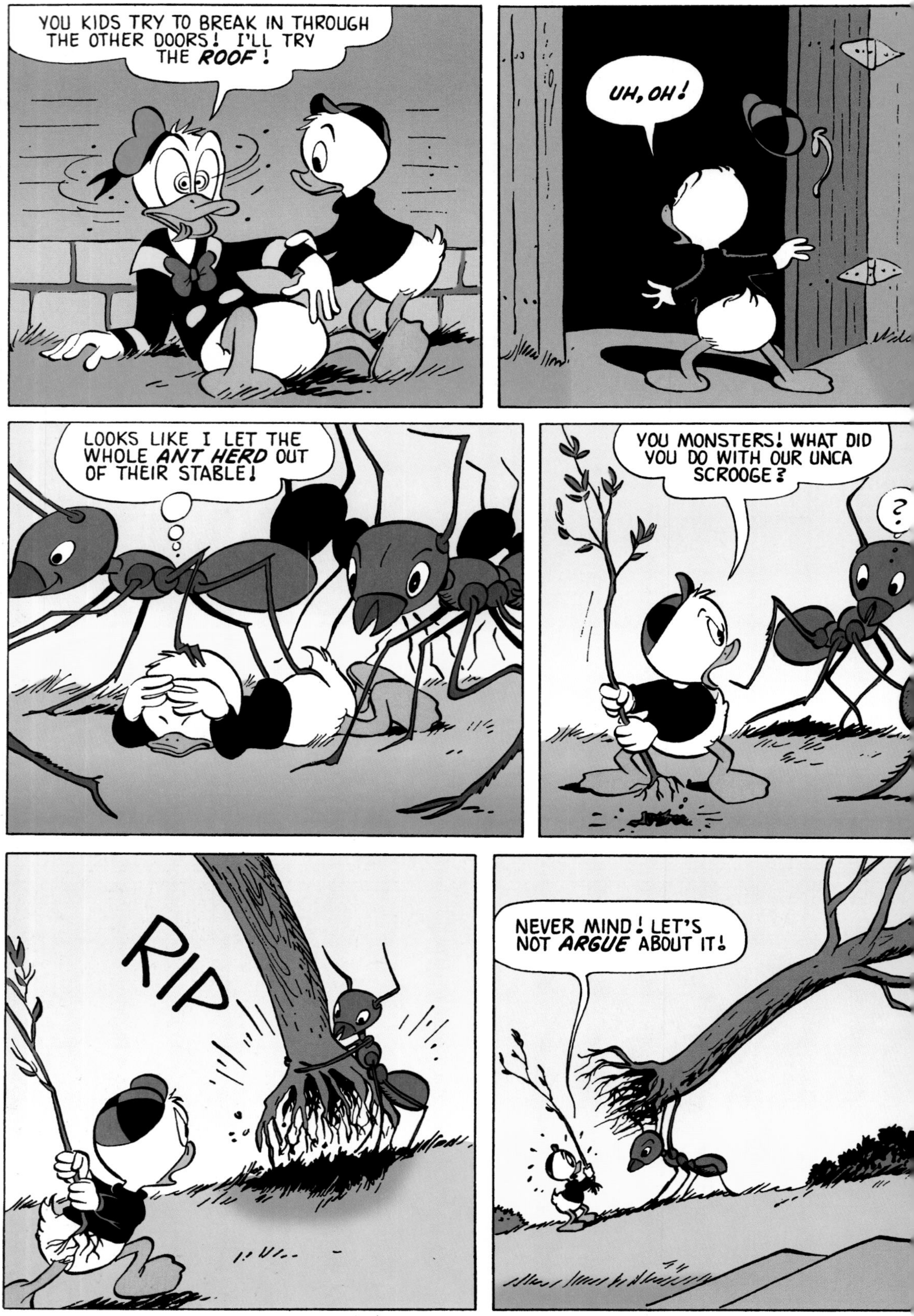
YOU KIDS TRY TO BREAK IN THROUGH THE OTHER DOORS! I'LL TRY THE ROOF!
UH, OH!
LOOKS LIKE I LET THE WHOLE ANT HERD OUT OF THEIR STABLE!
YOU MONSTERS! WHAT DID YOU DO WITH OUR UNCA SCROOGE?
?
RIP
NEVER MIND! LET'S NOT ARGUE ABOUT IT!

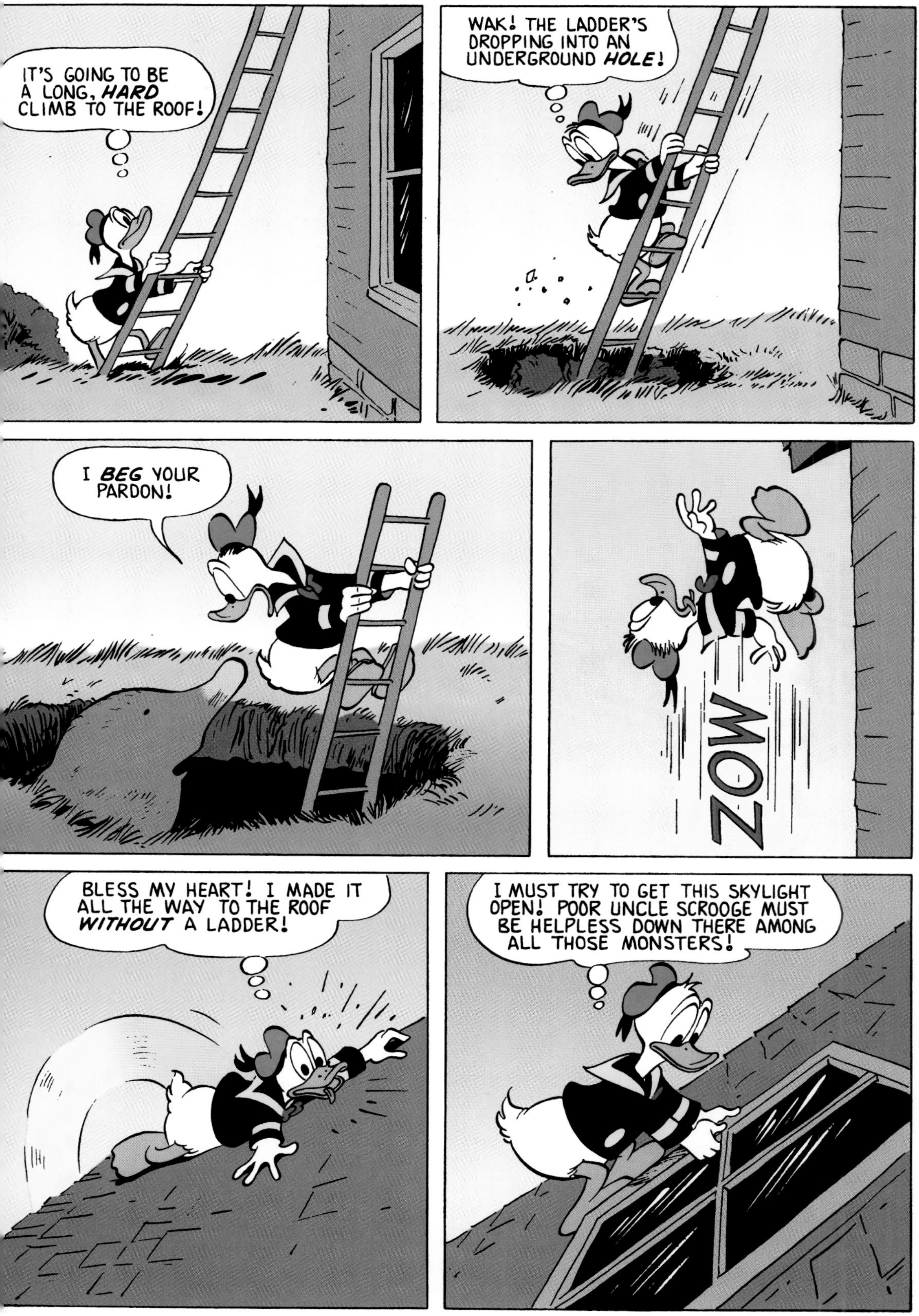
IT'S GOING TO BE A LONG, HARD CLIMB TO THE ROOF!
WAK! THE LADDER'S DROPPING INTO AN UNDERGROUND HOLE!
I BEG YOUR PARDON!
ZOOM
BLESS MY HEART! I MADE IT ALL THE WAY TO THE ROOF WITHOUT A LADDER!
I MUST TRY TO GET THIS SKYLIGHT OPEN! POOR UNCLE SCROOGE MUST BE HELPLESS DOWN THERE AMONG ALL THOSE MONSTERS!

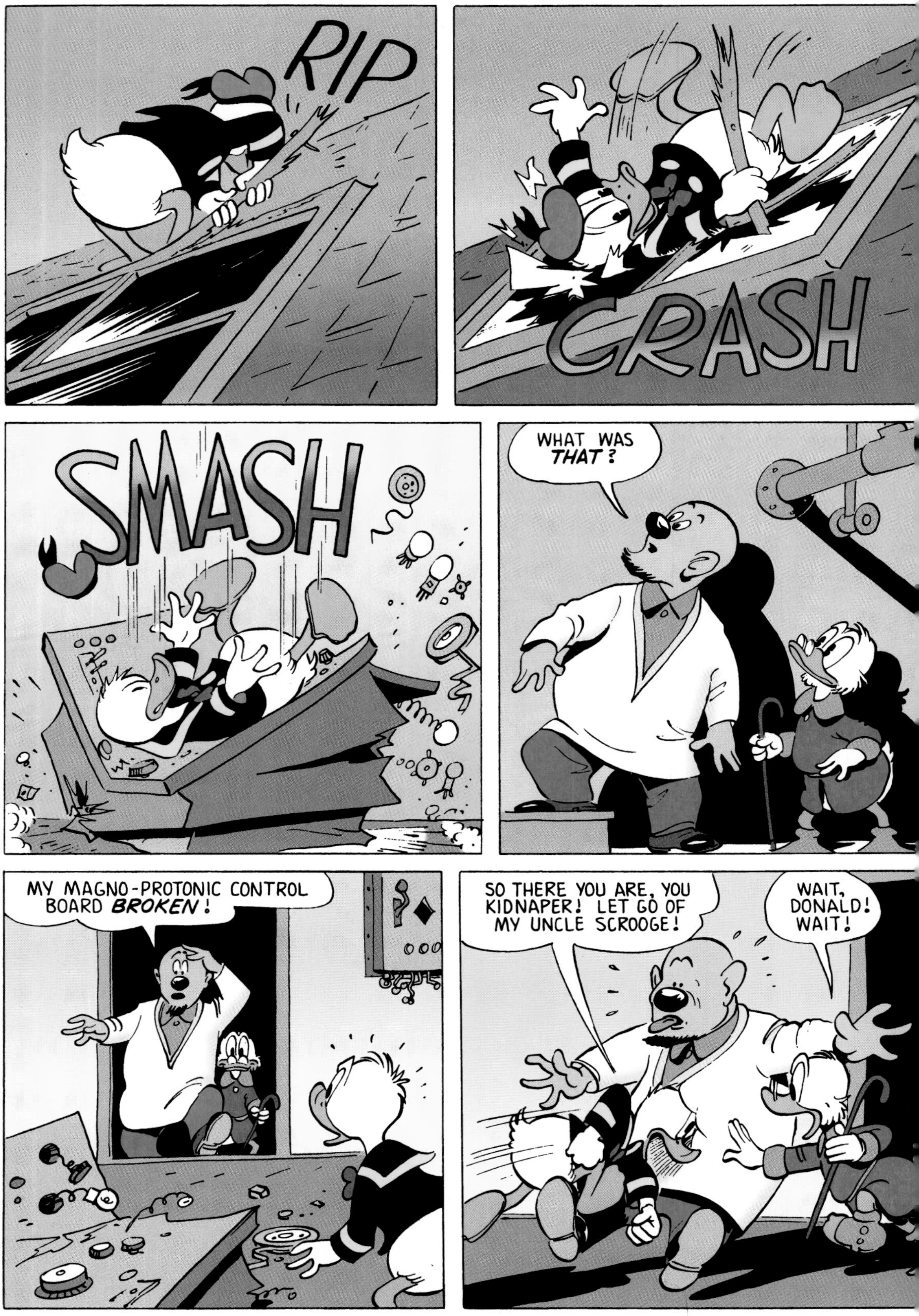

RIP
CRASH
SMASH
WHAT WAS THAT?
MY MAGNO-PROTONIC CONTROL BOARD BROKEN!
SO THERE YOU ARE, YOU KIDNAPER! LET GO OF MY UNCLE SCROOGE!
WAIT, DONALD! WAIT!

YOU'RE MAKING A MISTAKE, DONALD! THE DOCTOR DOESN'T HAVE *ME* IN HIS POWER — I HAVE *HIM*!

THIS CONTRACT WE'VE JUST SIGNED GIVES ME FIRST CLAIM ON THE SERVICES OF *ANY* ENLARGED CREATURES HE MAKES!

BUT I WON'T BE MAKING ANY FOR A LONG TIME, MR. McDUCK! MY PROTONIC CONTROLS ARE SMASHED!

I CAN'T MAKE ANY MORE ENLARGEMENTS FOR WEEKS! AND, WORSE YET, I CAN'T *SHRINK* THE CREATURES I'VE ALREADY ENLARGED!

MAGNO, THE *MOLE*, AND THE TITANIC *ANTS*!

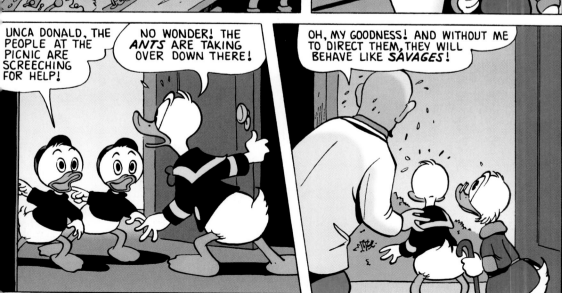

UNCA DONALD, THE PEOPLE AT THE PICNIC ARE SCREECHING FOR HELP!

NO WONDER! THE *ANTS* ARE TAKING OVER DOWN THERE!

OH, MY GOODNESS! AND WITHOUT ME TO DIRECT THEM, THEY WILL BEHAVE LIKE *SAVAGES*!

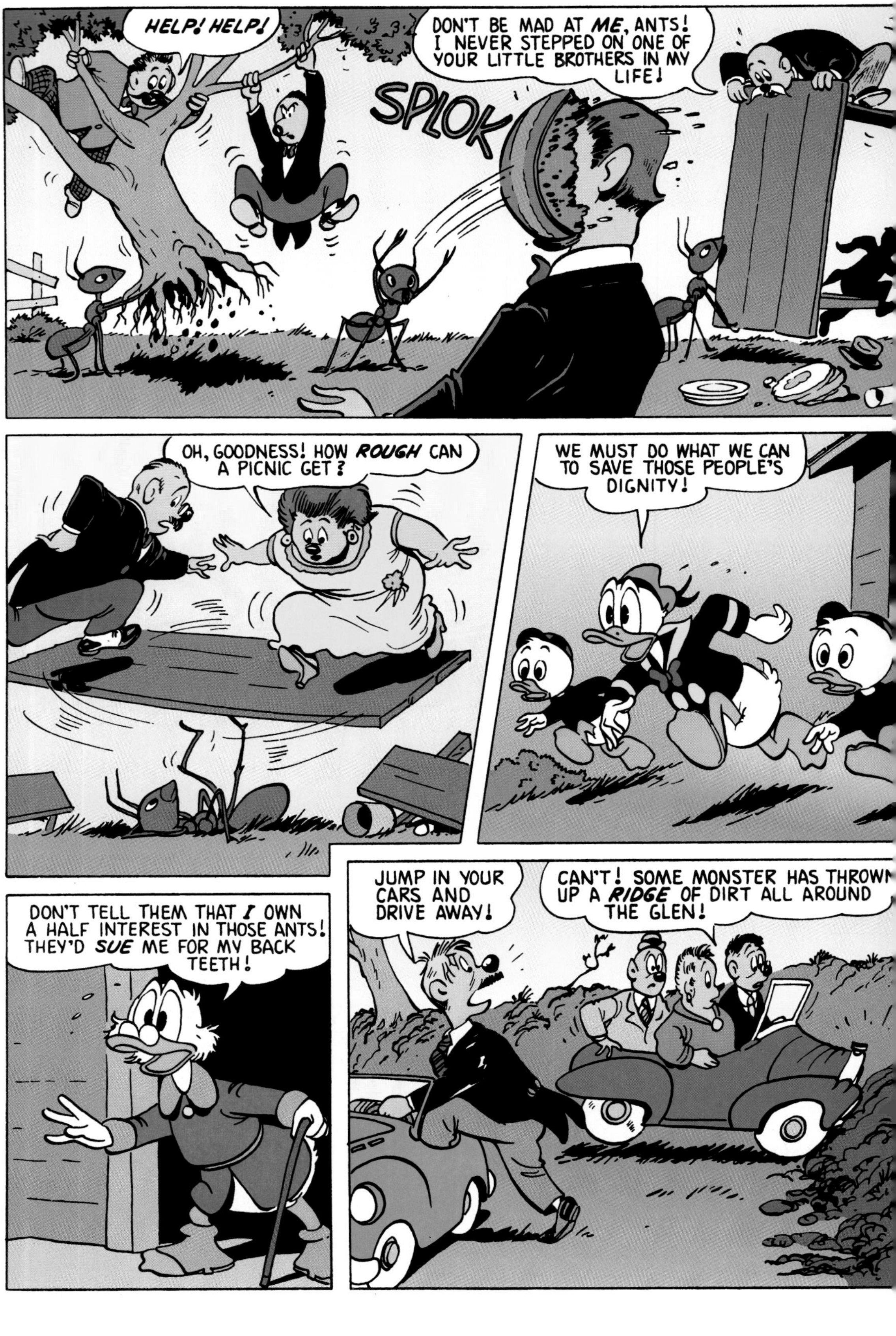
HELP! HELP!
DON'T BE MAD AT *ME*, ANTS! I NEVER STEPPED ON ONE OF YOUR LITTLE BROTHERS IN MY LIFE!
SPLOK
OH, GOODNESS! HOW *ROUGH* CAN A PICNIC GET?
WE MUST DO WHAT WE CAN TO SAVE THOSE PEOPLE'S DIGNITY!
DON'T TELL THEM THAT *I* OWN A HALF INTEREST IN THOSE ANTS! THEY'D *SUE* ME FOR MY BACK TEETH!
JUMP IN YOUR CARS AND DRIVE AWAY!
CAN'T! SOME MONSTER HAS THROWN UP A *RIDGE* OF DIRT ALL AROUND THE GLEN!

EEK

CHEER UP, MRS. GOLDWAD! I SAVED YOU SOME TRUFFLES!

KEEP THEM! I'M *STILL* WAITING FOR THE SALT AND PEPPER!

IT'S NO USE FIGHTING, BOYS! THE ANTS ARE GOING TO OVERRUN THE COUNTRYSIDE!

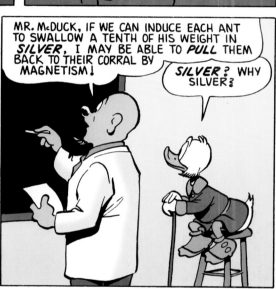

MR. McDUCK, IF WE CAN INDUCE EACH ANT TO SWALLOW A TENTH OF HIS WEIGHT IN *SILVER*, I MAY BE ABLE TO *PULL* THEM BACK TO THEIR CORRAL BY MAGNETISM!

*SILVER?* WHY SILVER?

MY MAGNETRONIC ATTRACTER WILL ONLY WORK ON THAT METAL!

MAYBE WE CAN USE *TABLE SILVER!*

NO! IT MUST BE *COIN* SILVER! DO YOU KNOW WHERE WE CAN FIND SOME *COINS* QUICKLY? *VERY* QUICKLY!

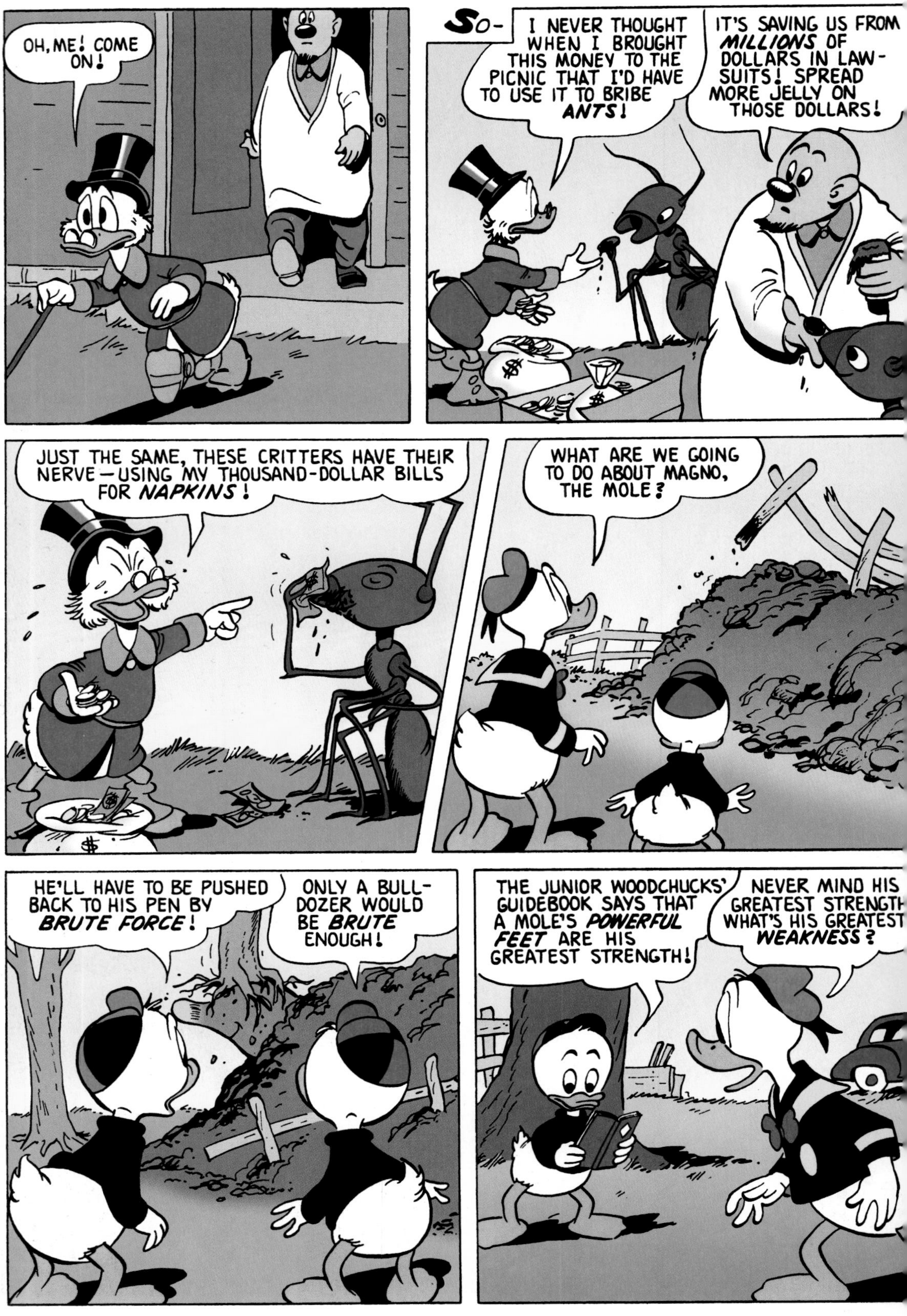
OH, ME! COME ON!
SO-
I NEVER THOUGHT WHEN I BROUGHT THIS MONEY TO THE PICNIC THAT I'D HAVE TO USE IT TO BRIBE ANTS!
IT'S SAVING US FROM MILLIONS OF DOLLARS IN LAW-SUITS! SPREAD MORE JELLY ON THOSE DOLLARS!
JUST THE SAME, THESE CRITTERS HAVE THEIR NERVE—USING MY THOUSAND-DOLLAR BILLS FOR NAPKINS!
WHAT ARE WE GOING TO DO ABOUT MAGNO, THE MOLE?
HE'LL HAVE TO BE PUSHED BACK TO HIS PEN BY BRUTE FORCE!
ONLY A BULL-DOZER WOULD BE BRUTE ENOUGH!
THE JUNIOR WOODCHUCKS' GUIDEBOOK SAYS THAT A MOLE'S POWERFUL FEET ARE HIS GREATEST STRENGTH!
NEVER MIND HIS GREATEST STRENGTH WHAT'S HIS GREATEST WEAKNESS?

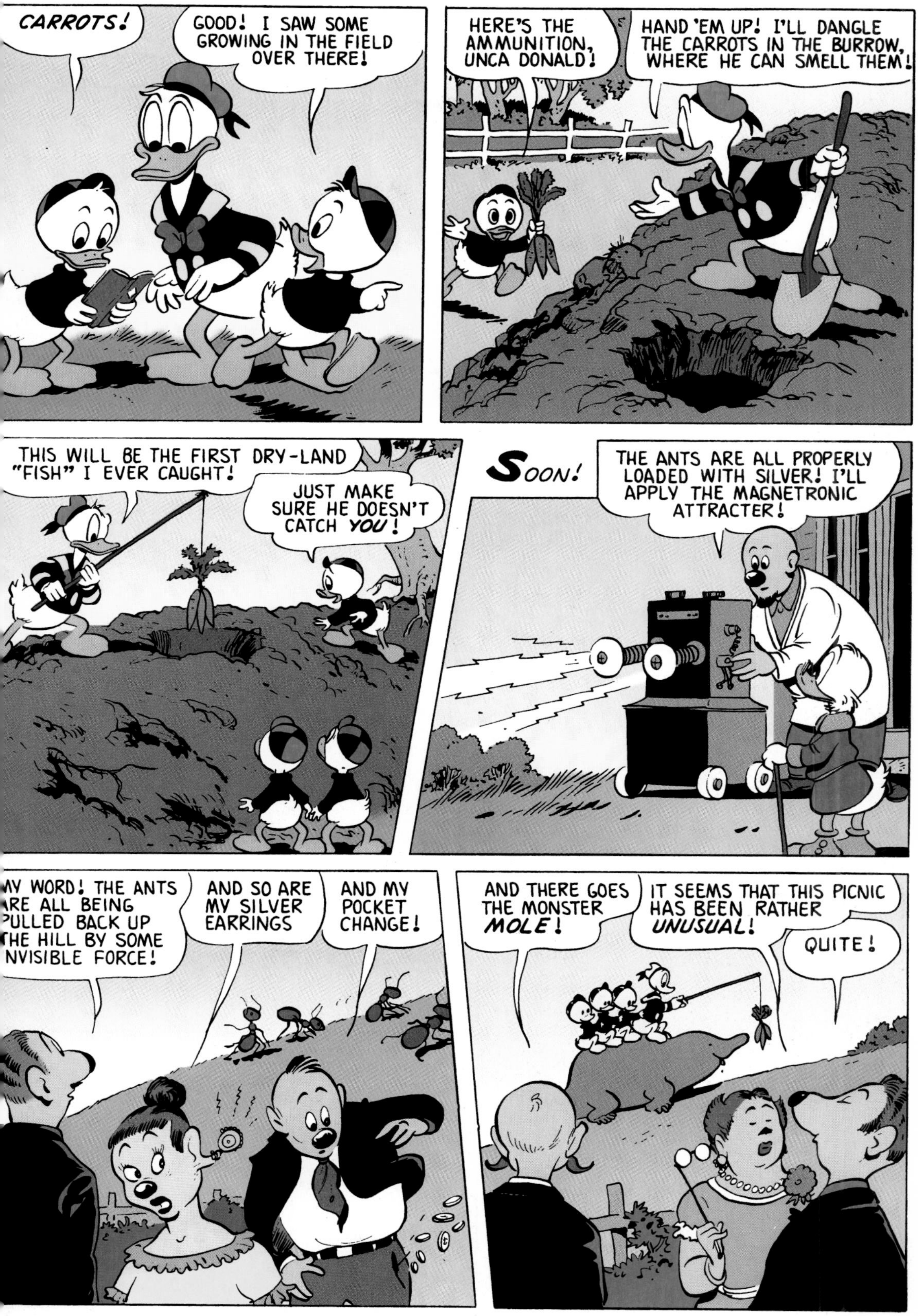
CARROTS!
GOOD! I SAW SOME GROWING IN THE FIELD OVER THERE!
HERE'S THE AMMUNITION, UNCA DONALD!
HAND 'EM UP! I'LL DANGLE THE CARROTS IN THE BURROW, WHERE HE CAN SMELL THEM!
THIS WILL BE THE FIRST DRY-LAND "FISH" I EVER CAUGHT!
JUST MAKE SURE HE DOESN'T CATCH YOU!
SOON!
THE ANTS ARE ALL PROPERLY LOADED WITH SILVER! I'LL APPLY THE MAGNETRONIC ATTRACTER!
Y WORD! THE ANTS RE ALL BEING ULLED BACK UP HE HILL BY SOME NVISIBLE FORCE!
AND SO ARE MY SILVER EARRINGS
AND MY POCKET CHANGE!
AND THERE GOES THE MONSTER MOLE!
IT SEEMS THAT THIS PICNIC HAS BEEN RATHER UNUSUAL!
QUITE!

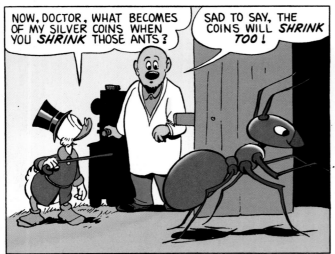

NOW, DOCTOR, WHAT BECOMES OF MY SILVER COINS WHEN YOU *SHRINK* THOSE ANTS?

SAD TO SAY, THE COINS WILL *SHRINK* TOO!

HUH? TWO MILLION, TWO THOUSAND AND SEVENTY-FIVE DOLLARS *DOWN THE HATCH!*

I'M SORRY, MR. McDUCK, BUT WHEN I'VE REPAIRED THIS ENLARGER, YOU'LL GET THAT ALL BACK — AND *MORE!*

(SOB! SOB! SNIFF ♪)

HOW? IN STEVEDORE *ANTS?* IN *FLIES* BIG ENOUGH TO CARRY AIRMAIL?

NO! IN SOMETHING *BIGGER* AND *BETTER* STILL!

I'VE DREAMED UP A *MOSQUITO* THAT CAN DRILL *OIL WELLS!*

*A*ND SO—

IT'S LUCKY ANNIE IS STILL GENTLE UNCLE SCROOGE IS TOO *OVERCOME* TO WALK BACK TO THE PICNIC!